Personas and Places: Negotiating Myths, Stereotypes and National Identities

Edited by
Jackie Raphael and Celia Lam

WH
WATERHILL
PUBLISHING

ISBN 978-0-9939938-9-3

Contents

PART III: Representing Gender and Nations

List of Contributors

Dr. Jo Coghlan is a Senior Lecturer in Sociology at the University of New England. Her research interest is in representations, frames and agency of the female political body. She has previously examined the female political personas of former Indonesian President Megawati Sukarnoputri, Australian politician Pauline Hanson and US presidential candidate Hillary Clinton.

Ellen Finlay has a Masters of International Relations from the University of Sydney and a Bachelor of Arts Double Major in Politics and Sociology with First Class Honours in International Relations from the University of Notre Dame Australia. She is currently at the University of NSW where she hopes to complete a PhD in the research area of healthy ageing across the Australian population.

Belinda Glynn is a doctoral candidate at Monash University. Her research examines negotiation and agency in relation to female stars in classical Hollywood.

Kerstin Hacker is a Senior Lecturer at Cambridge School of Art, Anglia Ruskin University and an Honorary Fellow of the Centre for the Understanding of Sustainable Prosperity. She is a photographer and academic and explores the concept of visual self-governance through practice research. Her ongoing work in Zambia *Generation Z* is the focus of her chapter in this volume.

Dr. Celia Lam is Assistant Professor in Media and Cultural Studies at the University of Nottingham Ningbo China. Her research focuses on the intersections between fan and celebrity cultures, and identity. She is an advisory board member of CMCS, and co-editor of *Credibility and the Incredible: Disassembling the Celebrity Figure* (2018) and *Becoming Brands: Celebrity, Activism and Politics* (2017).

Dr. Angelique Nairn is a Senior Lecturer in Communication studies at Auckland University of Technology in New Zealand. She specialises in teaching creative industries and media communication. Her research interests include organisational identity and identification, religion, sports management, celebrity studies, creative work and the business of creativity.

Dr Frances Nelson is a Senior Lecturer in Communication studies at Auckland University of Technology in New Zealand where she specialises in teaching creative industries. Her research interests include organisational communication and culture, power and control, creative work and the business of creativity, and the environment.

Dr. Melanie Piper teaches at the University of Queensland, Australia, in Film, Television, and Media studies. Her PhD dissertation, completed in 2017, focused on the adaptation of public personas to fictionalized characters in a range of screen media. She is currently working on revising her dissertation for a book manuscript.

Dr. Jackie Raphael teaches at Curtin University and focuses her research on endorsements and bromances. She is on the advisory board of CMCS and the *Celebrity Chat* producer. She has published various papers and books such as *Bridging Gaps in Celebrity Studies* (2016), *and Becoming Brands: Celebrity, Activism and Politics* (2017).

Dr. Louise St Guillaume currently works as a Lecturer and Discipline Coordinator of Sociology in the School of Arts and Sciences, the University of Notre Dame Australia. Louise is the 2011 winner of the Australian Critical Race and Whiteness Studies e-journal essay competition (non-Indigenous submission). Her current research interests include disability, income support, asylum/ refugee and Indigenous policy in Australia. She also has an interest in celebrity studies with her research in this area particularly focused on intersections of race and disability with celebrity.

Foreword to Personas and Places: Negotiating Myths, Stereotypes and National Identities

Sean Redmond

National Celebrity

Celebrity culture exists, in part, through intersecting forms of signification and as over-arching and textually specific discursive formations. Celebrities often stand as perfected or flawed creatures, extraordinary and ordinary at the same time; embody identity politics in and around gender, race, class, and sexuality; and give powerful meaning to the imagined body of the nation state. Celebrities are called upon to both 'glue' the social imaginary together and to outwardly represent what the nation state wants to be seen it is made of.

In relation to Ireland, for example, Moynagh Sullivan (2007) suggests:

> British bands such as the Spice Girls or Take That were openly patriotic in their iconography and in their dress, manufactured Irish bands, such as Boyzone and Westlife, who stormed the Irish and British markets in the 1990s and the early years of this decade, never draped themselves in the tricolour nor riverdanced. So although the boy bands appear, in contrast, innocently apolitical, they implicitly perform not only the newfound success of Celtic Tiger Ireland, but also the reasons for that success (p. 184)

Diane Negra makes a similar argument, when analyzing the star images of Sonja Henie and Shirley Temple, but the analysis here connects their white purity to national recovery, "an element that compensated for the sense of diminished national, white vigour in the 1930s" (Negra, 2001, p. 90). As Richard Dyer notes, Marilyn Monroe transmitted what it was like to be a perfected white woman in a 1950s America dealing with racial difference, and growing female independence (1987). Monroe created the somewhat contradictory 'experience' of desirable white womanhood for an America undergoing radical social and political transformation. Her body moved freely, it registered as soft and appealing, the embodiment of girl-like optimism and white womanly sensuality.

National celebrity can of course move us to global connectivity. In Pramod Nayar's (2015) recent work, celebrity and national identity can be infused with the vernacular of charity and benevolence:

> Brand Bollywood Care (BBC for convenience) helps reframe India as a global nation state suffused with benevolent ethics, retaining yet subtly erasing racial, national and geopolitical identifications by merging with, in distinctive fashion, transnational organizations like the United Nations or People for the Ethical Treatment of Animals. (p. 273)

However, Pramod is also at pains to express that a certain amount of legitimacy accrues to BBC due to its vernacular origins and roots. He uses the term "vernacular" fully alert to its racial and imperial roots, and to signal a binary with the 'global' interface. As he suggests, "care and charity work are technologies of global citizenship for the Bollywood star. They are conduits of hope and bring hope wherever their benevolence travels" (2015, p. 273).

Transnational stardom occupies a similar position in the global-local geopolitical space. Film stars can operate both as national and nationalist figures of identity – types of 'social glue' as noted above – and as international 'de-nationalized' entities that speak to and resonate with global audiences. For example, in terms of Hollywood, Elizabeth Ezra and Terry Rowden (2006) argue that star actors such as Russell Crowe, Kate Winslet, Jude Law, Penelope Cruz and Antonio Banderas function or operate as transnational stars, engaging in a "performance of Americanness" which is "increasingly becoming a 'universal' or 'universalizing' characteristic in world cinema" (2006, p. 2).

Russell Crowe: Transnational Ocker?

Russell Crowe is a fascinating example of the issues at play when thinking about national celebrity and transnational stardom: he occupies a cultural space when it comes to Australian film stars who are successful in mainstream Hollywood and American auteur cinema, and in Australian (made and set) films. The longevity of this career and the range of Hollywood and auterist films he has appeared in, suggest a star-actor who can straddle popularist and niche, commercial and artistic terrains. That Crowe is also a national and transnational actor also points towards a mutability and semiotic transferability that allows him to cross cultural borders with relative ease. He is national icon one day, and a figure beyond national borders the next.

Crowe is a remarkable example of the star-actor import and export business: home-grown Australian talent, crafted in part out of national archetypes and identity tropes; and an internationalist figure, able to transcend (de-odorize) his Australianness in the US and global marketplace. He is touched by the glitz and glamour of tinsel town and yet, he is one of Australia's own prodigal sons.

What is equally fascinating, however, is how Crowe's international success is also 'imported' back into Australia both to validate his talent and the value of Australianness, and to carry forward the signifiers of white-centric Hollywood stardom. Crowe re-enters Australian screen culture as a transnational fusion figure, simultaneously national and international, Australian and American, brute and cultured, ideally white and ordinary, and successful at home and abroad. Crowe's Australianness is 'here' and 'there' and this embodied fusion speaks to the way contemporary white masculinity plays out in contemporary Australia.

Crowe seems to be the personification and carrier of one of the dominant forms of Australian masculine identity: "He is perceived as an 'authentic man', a model of traditional values, a pre-feminist, anti- commodified or anti-metrosexual 'man's man'" (Gottschall, 2014, p. 863). For example, his involvement with the rugby league football team, the South Sydney Rabbitohs, connects him to a range of Australian signifiers and again places him in a male environment in deeply homosocial and parochial relationships. The widely circulated photograph of Crowe in an intense embrace with team captain Sam Burgess, after the Sydney Rabbitohs won the Australian NRL, places him within mateship type scenarios.

Connected to this, however, is the story of the underdog, played out in multiple ways: Crowe was the underdog actor who made it big in Hollywood; The Rabbitohs were the underdog footy team, on the verge of extinction, who Crowe helped re-build and resurrect, his own rags to riches story cementing the low to high mythology of the team. Setting this fable within settler and foundation myths, and one can see how Crowe is a national icon, capturing the qualities of white Australia and the battlers and achievers who make their way.

In this frame, Crowe exists in two cross-connecting representational streams: he is a Hollywood star who lives out the American Dream; and he is the Australian boy next door who is safely one of us. Crowe is in the ideological import/export business: his star image seamlessly moving across divergent national and international spaces. In a contemporary setting, where migration and immigration and indigenous identity unmake this myth, Crowe becomes a form of nationalist social glue. And yet again, not quite.

Crowe is an outsider, born in New Zealand, with a residence in Beverley Hills, whose left-centred politics is well known (he supported Julia Gillard in the 2012 'spill' vote). Crowe's ideological and cultural allegiances are full of fault lines and tensions, in the same way that his star image is. In a very real sense he embodies the complexities of modern global relations. *Cinderella Man* (Howard, 2005), for example, while being set in depression hit America, clearly speaks to the coming GFC and the austerity politics it unleashed across the globe. Crowe's James J. Braddock, a labourer by day, is everyman set against corporate greed and an uncaring social system. This is a political message that is easily if vexedly imported into Australia.

Crowe's first directorial feature, *The Water Diviner* (2014) perhaps best sums up his contradictory and unravelling ideological function within this contemporary nationalist maelstrom. In an interview about the film he responds, "Growing up in Australia, you tend to see the battle from only one point of view," Crowe says. "I wanted to have the audience realize from the first take, 'Oh, this is not my grandfather's Gallipoli'" (Giamatti, 2005).

The Water Diviner tells the story of an Australian farmer, Joshua Connor, played by Crowe, who loses his three sons at Gallipoli and travels there four years later to find their bodies. On one level, the film draws upon all the masculine qualities of the Crowe star-character image: he is a "paragon of manhood" (D'Addario, 2015), wanting to return his sons to their rightful resting place and honour their sacrifice.

Crowe's character is given the power of insight: he can find water in the desert and this clairvoyance also enables him to find his sons, as if it is his manifest destiny to do so. On another level, however, the film is critical of the 'masculinity' and nationalist fervour of the Gallipoli landings, one of Australia's foundational 'mateship' myths. The film in part characterizes the Gallipoli campaign as an unprovoked invasion of a sovereign Nation State, and offers us access to the Turkish point of view, allowing audiences to also see the suffering they experienced. There are clear global markers here, not least the forced invasion of Iraq. However, one can also see the film as an allegory about the white settlers' invasion of Australia at the 'birth' of the modern nation state.

What Crowe's star image reveals is probably the unstable state of the nation, blinded by its settler past, holding onto its foundational myths, and yet forcefully aware of their limitations and of their past-tenseness. Australia is at a crossroad, the right wanting to set up borders and keep out undesirables, and the left wanting to re-navigate and recast what the nation state is. Australia is very much set within the mirroring fantasy of Crowe's unstable star image. At the level of stardom, de-odorized star images work globally and yet they also retain and maintain their national(ist) inflections; as import and export exercises they move representations, dreams, ideologies across the globe and closer to home.

Bridging Gaps

The inflections and directions taken in this wonderfully exciting and innovative collection speak very much to the threads I have pulled together above. The volume does indeed bridge the gaps between nation and the transnational, the imaginary and the bodied, and the historical and contemporary. The authors collected here offer us a series of fascinating case studies that take us from the migrant and settler shores of Australia to the American success myth, from the biopic of Jackie Kennedy to the dresses of Michelle Obama, and from colonial myths, New Zealand celebrity activism, to the photographic representations of Zambia.

National celebrity in this collection is fleshed, spatial, and political, enabling the reader to explore the way celebrity has worked and continues to work in shaping and mapping the affective ideologies of nation states. What is particularly impressive is the way dominant media nations are juxtaposed across minority nation states, so the reader can readily access the way power is exercised and channelled in the present and across contemporary media history.

Case studies include a star analysis of Chris Hemsworth, in some ways a mirroring figure for Russell Crowe; an astute new reading of the star image of Cary Grant; an exploration of two former Presidential Ladies, Jackie O and Michelle Obama, who if read comparatively, demonstrate the way history, cultural memory, gender and ethnicity have shaped the American Dream; case study analysis of three Australian national stars, Stan Grant, Adam Hills, Dami Im, each of whom exist on the cultural margins, allowing the authors to demonstrate how celebrity culture creates zones of exclusivity within the national imaginary; a post-colonial reading of how Zambia is photographically represented through a surveying gaze that very often Others its borders; and an advocacy reading of New Zealand filmmaker Taika Waititi's support for the Human Rights Campaign "Give nothing to racism". Taken together they are a timely and important set of chapters that takes our understanding of national celebrity into vital new areas of analysis.

Sean Redmond, February 2018

References

Howard, R. (Director). (2005). *Cinderella man* [Motion picture]. United States: Universal Pictures

Crowe, R. (2014). *The water diviner* [Motion picture]. Australia: RatPac Entertainment

D'Addario, D. (2015, April 24). Daniel. 2015. Russell Crowe's The water diviner falls short. *Time Entertainment*. Retrieved February 5, 2018, from http://time.com/3833935/the-water-diviner-review-russell-crowe/

DeAngelis, M. (2008). Cinderella man: Russell Crowe as Il Diva, *Camera Obscura, 23* (1. 67), 47-67.

Dyer, R. (1987). *Heavenly bodies: Film stars and society*. London: Macmillan.

Ezra, E., & Rowden, T. (Eds.). (2006). *Transnational cinema: The film reader*. London: Routledge.

Giamatti, P. (2005). Russell Crowe. *Interview Magazine*. Sandra J. Brant Publisher. 83-89.

Gottschall, K. (2014). Always the larrikin: Ben Mendelsohn and young Aussie manhood in Australian cinema, *Continuum, 28*(6), 862-875.

Negra, D. (2001). *Off-White Hollywood: American culture and ethnic female stardom*. London: Routledge.

Sullivan, M. (2007). Boyz to Men: Irish boy bands and mothering the nation. In W Balzano., A. Mulhall & M. Sullivan (Eds.), *Irish postmodernisms and popular culture* (pp. 184-196). London: Palgrave Macmillan.

Nayer, P. K. (2015). Brand Bollywood care: Celebrity, charity and vernacular cosmopolitanism. In P.D. Marshall & S. Redmond (Eds.), *The Wiley companion to celebrity* (pp. 273-288), Hoboken: Wiley.

Introduction: Representations and (Mis)representations

Jackie Raphael and Celia Lam

The significance of celebrity studies lies, in part, in its capacity to interrogate, to negotiate and to critique that complex entity known broadly as 'society'. Within its multifaceted manifestations of culture (and cultures), societies define, and re-define themselves. They construct meanings around (and through) which its members locate sites of identification and signification. As high profile individuals possessive of signifying potential, celebrities represent issues that are both micro and macro in nature; simultaneously embodying both the personal and national. They are, in the words of Sean Redmond in the Foreword to this volume, "called upon to both 'glue' the social imaginary together and to outwardly represent what the nation state wants to be seen it is made of" (p. 1).

The chapters in this volume reflect on the role and function of celebrity figures and media representations thereof to uphold and challenge national imaginaries. Through a series of case studies, this book explores the intersections between representations of places and people. It interrogates the methods through which national myths are constructed, and examines the limitations of national identities. It offers critical reflection on the issues of race, gender, and disability/ability in the national imaginary of nations such as Australia, the United States, New Zealand and Zambia.

Personas and Places

This book is divided into three key sections: Part I: (Mis)representing Countries and Cultures, Part II: Representing People and Society, and Part III: Representing Gender and Nations. Part I offers critical analysis on racial representation. Jackie Raphael and Celia Lam analyze Chris Hemsworth's Tourism Australian Ambassador Campaign and its perpetuation of white and male-centric discourses in association with Australia identity. Kerstin Hacker explores globalized representations of Zambian culture that reinforce stereotypical discourses of Africa. Through her account of photographic representations by Zambian citizens, Hacker challenges the established narrative and offers a postcolonial image of Zambia. Both chapters suggest a need for change in the media representation of national cultures.

Part II of the book focuses on how famous identities embody and challenge existing notions of national identity. Louise St Guillaume, Ellen Finlay and

Celia Lam explore how a 'normalized' Australian identity is both reinforced and challenged by Australian celebrities who exist on the cultural margins of Australian society. Through case studies on Stan Grant, Adam Hills and Dami Im, representations of race and disability/ability in contemporary Australian identity are explored. Similarly, Angelique Nairn and Frances Nelson explore themes of race through their case study of New Zealand director Taika Waititi and the social campaign he led. These chapters broaden the issues of who the public are and how they are represented (or not represented) in the media by famous personas.

Part III explores themes of gender through case studies of Michelle Obama, the characterization of Jackie Kennedy in the film *Jackie* (2016), and Cary Grant. Each chapter investigates the connection between the celebrities' personas and the representation of America. Jo Coghlan focuses on how Obama's political status reimagines notions of womanhood in the United States. While Melanie Piper, examines the American myth and idealized notions of femininity through a character study of Jackie Kennedy. Belinda Glynn's analysis explores how the myth of the American Dream is used to recuperate the transgressive masculinity of the star persona of English-born Cary Grant. Overall, this book addresses themes of gender, race, culture, persona, myths and stereotypes, broadening the dialogue on national identity.

Acknowledgments

The editors wish to thank the Centre for Media and Celebrity Studies (CMCS) and the Centre for Ecological, Social & Informatics Cognitive Research (ESI.CORE) who sponsored the conference that inspired this book. They would also like to thank the authors for contributing to the volume and our reviewers – Bertha Chin, Ian Dixon, Nathan Farrell, Bethan Jones, Andrea Marshall and Kiera Obbard. Thanks to Professor Sean Redmond for providing the Foreword to this volume. Thanks also to Blake Cantrell for providing the illustration for the book cover.

References

Redmond, S. (2018). Foreword to personas and places: Negotiating myths, stereotypes and national identities. In J. Raphael & C. Lam. (Eds.), *Personas and places: Negotiating myths, stereotypes and national identities* (pp. 1-6). Toronto: WaterHill Publishing

Juan de Dios Larraín, J.dD. (Producer), & Larraín, P. (Director). (2016). *Jackie* [Motion picture]. United States: LD Entertainment

PART I:
(Mis)representing Countries and Cultures

Chris Hemsworth: Helping and hindering the Australian identity

Jackie Raphael and Celia Lam

Abstract. Chris Hemsworth represents Australia both when home and away. Through his portrayal of Thor in the Marvel Cinematic Universe films, Hemsworth is one of many Australians to have become a Hollywood A-lister. Externally, Hemsworth is viewed as a representation of Australia and the Australian identity, a notion reinforced through his selection as the 2016 Australian tourism ambassador. Hemsworth is often represented in media as a rugged and strong persona, a surfer who possesses the typical traits of larrikinism commonly associated with Australian stereotypes. This stereotype also tends towards representations of white Australia as the norm, and is influenced in no small part by the white washing of domestic and international media productions. Thus, while Australians are exposed to a narrative of multiculturalism internally, globally a white image of Australian identity persists. Additionally, the cultural emphasis on a larrikin persona perpetuates a male-dominated image. From Paul Hogan to Steve Irwin to Hugh Jackman and now Chris Hemsworth Australian identity is often associated with a specific form of masculinity. Footage from the tourism campaign featuring Hemsworth, re-imagines Australia as a serene and relaxed environment, compared to the rough outback previously portrayed. However, Hemsworth's image reinforces many pre-existing stereotypes. This paper explores the ways in which Hemsworth both develops the Australian identity and hinders it through stereotypes. Semiotic analysis of Tourism Australia's website reveals how Hemsworth's persona is constructed and functions within a tourism campaign for Australia.

Keywords: Chris Hemsworth, Australian national identity, Celebrity, Tourism.

Introduction

In 2016, Tourism Australia announced actor Chris Hemsworth as its ambassador, and followed this announcement with a series of advertisements featuring, firstly his voice and then his image. Hemsworth was reported to be a perfect fit for the campaign as he encapsulated Australia and an Australian identity. While Hemsworth was active in Australia for the early part of his career, it was not until his turn in Marvel Studio's *Thor* (Branagh, 2011), that he came to international attention. Hemsworth's association with Australia is thus fragmentary as his primary center of operation is in the United States. Yet, other aspects of his celebrity persona does make him amenable to association with a broader Australian identity. His laid-back larrikin persona, affection for outdoor activities and ability to 'retain' his Australian accent (albeit only off-screen), cloaks him in iconography stereotypically associated with the notion of 'Australian'. Through an analysis of his celebrity persona, and in particular his appearance in the Tourism Australia campaign, this chapter argues that while Hemsworth's image challenges some established constructions of Australian identity, he nonetheless reinforces and reaffirms a dominant discourse that features maleness and whiteness at its core.

Literature Review

Persona, Celebrity and Identity

Within celebrity studies, the celebrity figure is often considered for their symbolic potential: the ability for individuals to represent values and signify meanings. For Richard Dyer, the celebrity figure becomes a proxy for any and all individuals, through whom "personhood" is explored, as well as "the doubts and anxieties attendant on it" (Dyer, 1986, p. 6). The public visibility of such figures enables broader questions of identity construction to be associated with their images. Initially, these images are located within media of "primary circulation" (O'Shaughnessy & Stadler, 2012, p. 424), the films, television series and sporting fields where the celebrity figure is 'at work'. However, it is often in the media of "secondary circulation" (p. 424), the interviews, red carpet appearances and magazine articles, that the meanings around the celebrity figure are both consolidated and contested. In particular, the private and "off-stage" (Gledhill, p. 217) spaces of celebrity persona are of intense interest to media and fans alike, as it is imagined that within these spaces resides the 'authentic' or 'real' individual (Gamson, 1994; Holmes & Redmond, 2012). The construction of a celebrity figure is thus a combination of both public and private personas. It is a matrix of fictional, representational and individual narratives that together form a coherent persona.

Reflecting on the contemporary use of personalized (and social) media, David Marshall suggests that, rather than the representational culture of the broadcast era, celebrity figures construct a "public private self" (2010, p. 44) through the use of "presentational media" (p. 38). Through the integration of mediated presentations (photographs, videos, articles) and communicative practices (messages, comments and replies) celebrity figures commoditize their online personas through the creation and maintenance of their social media profiles (p. 42). Indeed, Marshall suggests that persona creation and maintenance is now a naturalized part of online culture, leading to "a spectrum of … public persona that in the past would have been an activity only engaged in by a quite limited celebrity and public personality culture" (2017, p. 68). Celebrity figures undoubtedly still occupy a position at the 'top' of the "specular economy" (Marshall, 2016, p.37). As such, their personas become attractive entities on which to attach commodities such as products and brands.

Celebrity personas hold a currency in the world, as their identities are easily recognizable, allowing them to communicate a message faster. As Grant McCracken (1989) explained in his term 'Meaning Transfer', a celebrity's brand is transferred to a product or service and then on to the consumer. This can also be reversed: the product being endorsed can help to reinforce a celebrity's brand. A celebrity persona is built over time through their careers, media interview, relationships and physical appearances. These then work as a shorthand, as their visual presence or voice in an advertisement can translate their brand to the brand being sold. The concept relies on the consumer believing in the message being communicated, and that the celebrity uses the product or service. When a consumer is also a fan, then the experience is heightened and the advertisement would become more powerful. A celebrity's capital varies depending on their level of fame and success. Their value is calculated based on their career but also on how relevant they are to the brand they are endorsing. Thus, meaning transfer only works if there is a connection between the two brands. This can then result in the celebrity capital creating economic capital. In the case of Chris Hemsworth's endorsement of Tourism Australia, the brand association operates with the intent of raising capital for the country through this use of Hemsworth's own capital.

Australian Identity

Discussions of Australian identity often focus on characterization, particularly on the gendered and racialized construction of an Australian national identity. Scholarship highlights the homogenous conception of 'Australian' that privileges a white-centric (more specifically, Anglo-Celtic) outlook. Some contributing factors to the emphasis on maintaining and preserving a white identity have been associated with Australia's colonial past, and its post-colonial immigration policies.

As a nation founded as a consequence of what Stephen Alomes describes as "the great excuse of Western imperialism" (1988, p. 209), anxiety persists over the contemporary nation's legitimacy and claims to land. Indeed, Ien Ang attributes the animosity of Hansonite politics to more than simply 'racism'. She suggests that "a '*spatial* anxiety' that is distinctive to Australia" (1999, p. 192) exists as a result of colonial land grabbing. This anxiety influences Australian concepts of itself, such that a fear of displacement from the land or any sense of 'home' provokes what Martin Crotty describes as a "siege mentality... [from a] perceived threat to white Australia's hold on the continent" (2001, p. 227). The reaction to this perception is a form of territorialism and racial protectionism, wherein a white identity is felt to require preservation. Writing about constructions of whiteness in Australian history, Ghassen Hage argues that anxieties over "living up to Whiteness" (2002, p. 402) not only have classed-based associations, they also place whiteness at the core of political and cultural constructions of Australian identity. Hage suggests that Australia, despite its multicultural immigration and social policies, still adopts a mostly white-centric outlook, such that public discourses on multiculturalism serve only to reinforce the dominance of the established white hierarchy (1998). The tension between characterizations of Australia as 'white' or 'multicultural' have roots in both historical and contemporary social and political policies. Hage outlines a period in recent Australian immigration history in which the construction of Australian identity was placed at a crossroads between a marginalized multiculturalism, and a multiculturalism "that displaces Anglo-Celtic culture to become the identity of the nation" (p. 427). The late 1970s and early 1980s saw the end of the 'White Australia' immigration policy (Department of Immigration and Border Protection, 2015, p. 48), and the adoption of multicultural social and immigration policies. The increasing presence of diverse cultures presented the possibility for the fostering of a national identity based upon hybridisation between newly arrived and more established cultures; what Hage describes as a "multicultural mainstream" (2002, p. 427). However, this mainstream did not did not eventuate (in the 1980s) due to a number of internal and global political factors such as increasing Asian immigration, financial insecurity, and the rise of anti-immigration political parties.[1]

The characterization of contemporary Australian identity is thus one in which multiple identities are subsumed beneath a dominant and homogenous (predominately white) identity. Writing of multiculturalism as it is manifest in the sport of soccer, Baker and Rowe suggest that in the Australian context, "the national 'we' characterizing national communities tends to be defensive rather than expansive … with belonging felt through similarity rather than difference" (p. 309).

A similar tension between ethnic and national identities is noted by Laura Moran in her recent (2016) exploration of young refugees at a Queensland high school. She noted that, while de-racialized modes of expression were encouraged, so too were 'appropriate' expressions of ethnicity that supported the broader discourses of diversity and tolerance within a multicultural society (Moran, 2016). Terming this discord as fluctuations between "discourses of

---

[1] See Hage (2002, pp. 430-434) for more on the contributing factors to shifts in the articulation of Australian multiculturalism, White paranoia and White decline.

integration and tolerance" (p. 709), Moran highlights the strategic use of markers of diversity within a social structure that is, ultimately, homogenous in nature. Indeed, Moran's work echoes Hage's 2002 assertion that Australian multiculturalism is one in which it is "a marginal reality in a mainly Anglo-Celtic society" (p. 427). Contemporary Australia, while adopting multicultural discourses, is one in which the centrality of whiteness is upheld.

Primacy of Masculinity in Australian National Identity

In addition to the centrality of whiteness in the dominant narrative of Australian identity, scholars have highlighted the mostly masculine nature of the nation's characterization. This has a legacy in the foundation myths of the contemporary Australian nation – from bush rangers (Tranter & Donoghue, 2008) to larrikins (Thompson, 2007) to ANZACs (Donoghue & Tranter, 2015) and other 'rugged' hyper-masculine models of masculinity (Hogan, 2010). The Australian identity becomes associated with a certain type of hyper-masculine masculinity that celebrates dominance, control and authoritarian disregard. Jackie Hogan characterizes Baz Luhrmann's 2008 film *Australia* as one in a continuum of narratives that defines the Australian national identity "by fetishising white Australian manhood and marginalizing women and non-white Others" (p. 63). The effect is the sidelining of non-white, non-male figures in the national imagination (Hogan, 2010). Within the *Australia* narrative, and others of similar ilk, male figures who fulfil traditional and heteronormative gender roles are constructed as heroes whose deeds are narratively (and by extension socially) valued above women and other ethnicities. The consolidation of a white male image of Australian identity it thus effected.

Indeed, Hogan (2010) makes this observation of the film *Australia:*

> To the international audience, Australia is being sold as a tourist destination, one 'where adventure and romance [is] a way of life,' … But Australians are … sold a comforting vision of the nation, one in which good triumphs over evil, in which ordinary men are heroes, in which men and women fit comfortably into traditional gender roles, and in which, with the exception of a few bad apples, people of diverse backgrounds harmoniously coexist. (p. 68)

The power of narrative, and the celebrity figure within the machinations of the creative industries, to represent, reflect and contribute to the national imaginary is both a product of contemporary celebrity culture, as well as a result of Australia's continued definition of itself. This chapter explores Australian actor Chris Hemsworth's role in Tourism Australia's 2016 campaign. The chapter argues that, while Hemsworth's celebrity persona may challenge some representations of masculinity, he reinforces others at the same time. Hogan observes *Australia* served to perpetuate a fetishized notion of Australian masculinity, and Australian identity. To a lesser degree, we argue that Hemsworth's involvement in the Tourism Australia campaign likewise perpetuates a particular image of Australian identity.

Case Study

Method

Chris Hemsworth's social media posts relating to the campaign were archived on the Tourism Australia website. It also included posts from Hemsworth's wife, Elsa Pataky. These were collected on October 30, 2017, and semiotic analysis was applied. Using Barthes theories, we broke down the details in each image and analyzed the wording of the captions. These details provided evidence of the tone of voice Hemsworth was attempting to convey in his endorsement of Australia. Pataky's posts were targeted at a Spanish audience, as the posts were written in her native language. Furthermore, there are multiple versions of the first video advertisement for global audiences. The shorter video of the Australian version was selected, as it had the most views online. Semiotic analysis was applied to this video also, so that cultural details could be identified. The common themes identified across both the video and social media suggest that Australia is predominantly Caucasian, filled with beaches, adventurous but family friendly and has a strong masculine tone. The issues relating to this identity are discussed throughout the case study, as well as how Hemsworth's persona aids the meaning transfer process in the endorsement.

Who is Chris Hemsworth?

Chris Hemsworth was born on 11 August, 1983 in Melbourne, Australia (IMDb, 2017). He has two brothers who also act, Liam and Luke. He married Spanish actress Elsa Pataky in 2010 and they have three children (IMDb, 2017). Hemsworth is best known for his role as Thor in the Marvel Universe franchise. Hemsworth is renowned as being funny, nice, charismatic and family-orientated. This identity has been built through his interview appearances and the way his peers talk about him. However, he also portrays a stereotypical 'Aussie bloke' who enjoys the outdoors and particularly speaks about surfing near his home in Byron Bay. His large stature and good looks often place him in heroic roles. This image is also what is used for various endorsements.

What is Hemsworth Selling?

Hemsworth has been used to sell a variety of brands including Tag Heuer watches, Hugo Boss perfume and Foxtel. His Tag Heuer endorsement links well with his role as a racecar driver in *Rush* (Howard 2013), much like how they used Steve McQueen posthumously in relation to his racing film *Le Mans* (Katzin 1971). Tag Heuer's brand relates to sports, efficiency, strength, durability and sophistication. By attaching himself to this brand, Hemsworth adopts some of these qualities while also transferring the meaning attached to his brand, which is cool, sexy and strong. Similarly, Hugo Boss is renowned as classy and this is reflected in the endorsement. In the *Man of Today* advertisement, Hemsworth is shown wearing a suit, attending meetings and speaking in a more professional tone of voice to match the tone of Hugo Boss' existing brand (BOSS, 2017).

On the other hand, the Foxtel campaign seems to rely predominantly on his good looks and is much more casual and comedic, as he is shown searching for his own movies on Foxtel (CBAustralia, 2016). Furthermore, he is in a singlet and shorts shaking his drink, which connects well with his fitness image. This also helps to reach the target audience, which is everyday Australians. While these brands are utilizing Hemsworth to sell their products, each of these endorsements add to his identity and are relatively consistent with the various facets of his image. This creates a mutual benefit in the meaning transfer process. However, a more significant campaign that Hemsworth has been attached to is for Australian tourism, as he is not just representing a brand, but a nation.

Hemsworth's global identity and stereotypical Australian persona make him a suitable match for this campaign. By selecting him as the ambassador they are utilizing his pre-constructed image and all of the connotations associated with him as a symbol of masculinity, sex-appeal, Hollywood status, friendliness, relaxed and much more. Tourism Australia Managing Director, John O'Sullivan stated; "Chris truly embodies the Australian way of life and his love of his home country, with all its natural beauty, makes him an ideal ambassador," (Tourism Australia, 2016). After living in the United States to build his career as an actor, Hemsworth moved his family back to Australia. This decision further reinforces his passion for the country, which works as a selling point. Furthermore, Hemsworth brought his work to Australia, as he requested that *Thor: Ragnarok* (Waititi 2017) be filmed close to his home, and by doing so he was able to create a cross promotion with a viral video of Thor and Hulk on vacation in Australia (moviemaniacsDE, 2016). Moreover, many Hollywood celebrities flew to Australia to produce the film, which generated a lot of media hype. However, Hemsworth's Hollywood image is not what sells Australia specifically, it is the credibility behind his storytelling when he reminisces about growing up in Australia.

Hemsworth is frequently asked about his childhood and he often reinforces certain Australian stereotypes. For example, Hemsworth has spoken about shooting his brother Liam with a BB gun as a child (Wigney, 2017). Liam has also reinforced this image, by sharing stories about throwing a knife at Chris's head when they were children (Team Coco, 2012). These stories build on the myth of hyper-masculine Australians who are tough and rugged. They have also spoken a lot about growing up surfing. During a recent interview Hemsworth stated "I love the 'shark-infested waters", explaining that he is cautious of the right times to surf but his heroic attitude again adds to the Australian myth of adventure (Wigney, 2017). Furthermore, Hemsworth has spoken about making the decision to move his family to Australia so his children could grow up in a similar way that he did, and that he specifically chose to be close to the beach (Goulopoulos & La Cioppa, 2016). This decision certainly adds credibility to his endorsement of the country.

These details have been used by Tourism Australia, as is evident in O'Sullivan's statement:

> From learning how to surf on Phillip Island, fishing with his brothers in the Northern Territory and family beach holidays, Chris has grown up in Australia in and around water and his own personal experiences bring a truly authentic and influential Australian voice to our campaign (2016).

This notion of "authenticity" is important to the campaign, as it is with any endorsement. However, when a celebrity is representing the country they were born and raised in, the credibility is far easier to reinforce than suggesting they use a particular product. It is important that the brand alignment is strong for the meaning transfer process to work accurately.

In the past, Australia has been associated with people such as Paul Hogan and Steve Irwin, who have represented more of a rugged outback identity. They also represented a sense of strength and adventurous danger. Hemsworth utilizes some of these qualities, but mainly reflects the relaxed, surfer image while also portraying a more typical 'Hollywood-handsome' image of Australian men.

Yet, his attractiveness was not used in the initial video advertisement, it relies purely on his voice-over. The campaign was accompanied with publicity announcing Hemsworth's new role, so people could easily make the connection. Hemsworth's involvement in the campaign also goes beyond this to include his social media posts.

Tourism Australia announced:

> Millions of Chris Hemsworth fans on Instagram, Twitter and Facebook will be able to follow the actor and his family on a recent family trip throughout Australia, as part of a Tourism Australia campaign to encourage more international travellers to book an Australian holiday (2016).

This element further reinforces the credibility of his role as ambassador, as he is actively becoming a tourist of his own country. He is also involving his family in these photographs, which shows a safe side to Australia. Yet, he contradicts this with more adventurous images, to appeal to everyone from daring explorers to those wanting a relaxed holiday. While they are clearly targeting Hemsworth's fans with the online part of the campaign, the television commercial is more relatable to a wider audience by excluding his visual presence. Overall, through the various aspects of the campaign, they are able to reach a broad range of people.

Campaign

The first video launched as part of the Hemsworth Tourism Australia campaign features Hemsworth's voice over describing the colors and feelings of Australia, while the footage shows landscapes and people enjoying the country. There is some cultural diversity, however the video is predominantly white. Only a few shots show indigenous culture, with a small number suggesting Australia's cultural diversity. The video ends with the tagline "There's nothing like Australia." Hemsworth's voice is dramatic throughout, which is well suited to the pace of the tranquil visuals and the song. The advertisement is sufficiently broad to be used anywhere in the world and has various adaptations for specific regions. This varies from the 1984 Paul Hogan advertisement for Australia, where he addressed America specifically in the opening (CrossMediaOwnership, 2009). Hogan also used comedy and Australian slang such as "fair dinkum", "Good'ay" and "shrimp on the Barbie". While this older advert also showed the beaches and wide-open landscape, it was very much focused on the image of Crocodile Dundee and his 'Aussie' language. This particular advertisement was whitewashed, not showing any indigenous culture or multiculturalism. Thus, the advertisements have certainly progressed over the years, however they are still selecting blonde-hair, masculine leading men as their ambassadors.

This is the image that international audiences already identify with Australia, thus using this myth helps to convey the message faster. As Barthes explained in his semiotic theories on denotation and connotation; "Signs and codes are generated by myths and in turn serve to maintain them" (Chandler,

2017). The advertisement thus, reinforces the existing myths of the attractive beach loving Australians. It is not false, but a hyperbole that generalizes the entire nation. Hemsworth is also used to personify Australia through his own visual identity. The hyper-masculine, adventurous myth solidified by Hogan and his role as Crocodile Dundee, is also reinforced by Hemsworth's large stature and persona.

A large difference between the Hemsworth and Hogan campaigns is the addition of social media. The images were used on the Tourism Australia website, along with quotes from Hemsworth about loving Australia, and links to lists that he had supposedly made: Hemsworth's itinerary; Hemsworth's top five favorite beaches; Hemsworth's top three experiences on Hayman Island; and Chris Hemsworth's Ultimate Coastal Holiday. These lists allow consumers to put trust in the suggestions made, as they are attached to Hemsworth's brand.

The images Hemsworth posted online show him predominantly with family and friends. His children's faces are never shown in order to protect them from the media, but Hemsworth and Pataky are shown regularly. By posting the somewhat personal pictures on his social media accounts, this adds credibility to the experiences he is sharing.

The series of images create a narrative depicting Australia as family friendly, romantic, relaxing and adventurous. For example, June 5 2016, Hemsworth posted an image of himself in front of Uluru calmly holding a snake. Adding to this masculine persona, June 7, 2016 Hemsworth posted an image of himself in a singlet and shorts in the bush with three other men, captioning it as a boys fishing trip. In contrast June 10, 2016 Hemsworth posted an image of him with his family enjoying Hayman Island during sunset. This conveyed a gentler image of Australia. Various other images were circulated online by Hemsworth, Pataky and Tourism Australia. Each of these images depicted various aspects of how Hemsworth enjoys Australia and provide different connotations for audiences to interpret. Through the meaning transfer process, these images suggest that tourists who follow Hemsworth's itinerary and advice online can also be like him – have fun adventures whether they are looking for a 'boys trip' or 'family bonding'.

Discussion

Overall, the endorsement was clearly a success, with reports stating the campaign "generated more than 2000 media stories worth the equivalent of $55 million in marketing dollars" (Ironside, 2016). The campaign thus reached a wide audience, both internationally and nationally. While the campaign re-characterizes Australia as a peaceful, natural and adventurous destination, it nonetheless conforms to pre-existing racialized (and gendered) discourses through its portrayal of Hemsworth.

Perpetuation of white-centric Discourses

Two government reports released in 2016 statically addresses the discrepancy between on-screen portrayals of Australia and the reality of the society represented. In August, Federal government agency Screen Australia, released findings of a landmark study focused on diversity on Australian screens. Although only featuring fictional productions, the findings revealed a predominately White representation (Screen Australia, 2016). With recent census data concluding "that nearly half of all Australians were either born overseas or had at least one parent who was born overseas" (Australian Bureau of Statistics, 2016), the Screen Australia finding confirmed what many in academia had long suggested; the racial diversity of Australia is absent from its onscreen representation of itself.

The media play an integral role in the construction of a nation's sense of identity. Following Benedict Anderson, in contemporary nation states a sense of belongingness is located not in the connections of a 'people' to a 'sovereign', but between members of the "imagined community" (2006, p.7). The image of the nation is where a sense of belonging and identity is located, and it is through the media that this image is constructed and disseminated. To this end, media representation of Australia (as white) is a reflection of a national identity that excludes a significant portion of the population from the national imagination.

As previously mentioned, the selection of celebrities for previous Tourism Australia campaigns tends to privilege Anglo-European celebrities (Paul Hogan a case in point). The selection of Hemsworth as the latest in a long line of Anglo-European celebrities reinforces the construction of a national image that is predominantly white. As tourism campaigns are designed primarily for international projection, the resulting effect is the construction of an external narrative that conflicts with the internal realities of a multicultural society. As a member of (a dominant) section of Australian society, Hemsworth undoubtedly represents Australia. However, he is positioned within the campaign as the embodiment of the potential visitor; offering vicarious experiences as he travels through Australia. Positioned thus, the campaign depicts Australia as a space that is experienced through the privileged gaze of a middle class white male. With an emphasis on beaches, nature and a sense of adventure the political complexities and social realities of the nation are circumvented. The aim of tourism campaigns is undoubtedly to market the nation as an attractive travel destination, and not to engage in socio-political debates. However, the (often idealized) depiction of the nation at once reveals, and contributes to, the dominant discourses that shape the national imagination.

Troubling Discourses Over Land

An ongoing discussion that this current campaign engages with is the issue of land ownership, and the tensions over land that has historically shaped Indigenous and non-Indigenous Australian relations. The use of the title 'Chris Hemsworth's Australia' as the headline of the Tourism Australia website contains two possible readings. Firstly, that the images of Australia presented on the site are sourced from Hemsworth's social media accounts, and thus represent *his* view of Australia. The creation of this sense of personalization appeals to the individualism of neoliberal discourses, and presumably also reflects the freedom of the Australian landscape.

An alternative reading of the title is located in a sense of ownership, of the land belonging to Hemsworth (and the 'mainstream' white Australia that he represents). While the advertisement and website do include images of Indigenous Australians showing tourists the Australian outback, these are limited and presented primarily through the perspective of the would-be-visitor, or Hemsworth. Problematically, claims of ownership directly challenge ongoing political discussions that aim to partially reconcile the disparity between Indigenous and non-Indigenous Australians by addressing the historical displacement of Indigenous peoples from their land. In 1992, the landmark Mabo High Court ruling overturned the notion of Terra Nullius[2] upon which European settlers legitimized their claim to Indigenous land. Since that time, the management of Indigenous lands continues to be a politically contentious issue. In particular, the use of Indigenous lands and sacred sites for tourism is debated. On the one hand, some profits from tourism do return to the Indigenous communities and enable a degree of self-sufficiency. On the other hand, the commercialization of tradition is viewed as disrespectful and culturally insensitive.

Thus, the campaign's depiction of the land as 'Hemsworth's Australia' appears to perpetuate outdated notions of non-Indigenous ownership of Australian land. At the very least, it engages with Ang's notion of "spatial

---

[2] Terra Nullius (meaning nobody's land), was a principle applied to Australia in the late 18th century to facilitate European settlement and claims to land. In 1982 Eddie Mabo, and four other Torres Strait Islanders started legal proceedings to establish native title; claims to traditional land ownership. In 1992 the High Court of Australia found in Mabo's favour, effectively overturning terra nullius in Australia.

anxiety" (1999, p. 192), in which the legitimacy of the nation's claim to land is questioned. Through its 'claim' to Australia by virtue of its textual positioning, the campaign (perhaps unknowingly) replicates discourses that reinforce racialized territorialism (Crotty, 2001).

Masculinity

The ruggedness of the outback male is often emphasized in depictions of Australian masculinity. As Jackie Hogan argues, the "fetishizing [of] white Australian manhood" (2010, p. 63) is prominent in Australian media such as the film *Australia* (Luhrmann, 2008) and its associated tourism campaign. Within this construct, Australian identity is linked to a specific type of masculinity: of men who fulfil traditional and heteronormative gender roles, whose locus is in the outside spaces of rural or outback Australia, and who are predominately white.

To a certain extent, Hemsworth challenges this mold as his depiction is less 'rugged'. Images that present Hemsworth as less aggressive construct an alternative form of masculinity to the hyper-masculine of previous Australian celebrities (such as Paul Hogan or Steven Erwin). As previously mentioned, one of the first images on the Tourism Australia website places Hemsworth in front of Uluru, cradling a snake. The image is a distinctly 'softened' one, as Hemsworth does not dominate the frame and adopts a demure countenance. The colder climate also counters the image of a 'harsh' Australian outback, which demands a 'tough' masculine outlook in order to survive. However, Hemsworth is holding a snake, an animal that is traditionally viewed as dangerous (and recalls the rugged masculinity of Crocodile Dundee). Thus, while the he is depicted as 'softer', the construction of this non-rugged masculinity fits within a broader 'rugged' and hyper-masculine context.

Other images of Hemsworth feature his child-rearing abilities. Images of Hemsworth with his children are posted by both Hemsworth and Pataky, thus presenting her view of him as part of the campaign and giving her a voice. While these images challenge traditional gender roles that assign child-rearing to women, the context of these images reaffirms other modes of masculinity. Hemsworth is depicted nurturing and caring for his children, however all the images locate this act in outdoor spaces; spaces removed from the domesticity (and interiority) of the home. Like the image of the snake, these spaces thus afford a degree of flexibility in the performance of masculinity, but firmly locate them within the confines of a masculine exterior space. The fact that the images depict Hemsworth schooling his male child in the sport of fishing (a masculine coded activity) further reinforces this construction.

Completing the construction of Hemsworth's masculinity are images that portray him as gregarious (with friends drinking beer), and enjoying the outdoors (in the outback), and images that emphasize his muscular physique (as he performs a martial arts move surrounded by nature). Thus, while the presentation of Hemsworth's masculinity does challenge notions of 'rugged' hyper-masculinity associated with the Australian male, it does so within the confines of that pre-existing masculine construction. In the words of Hogan, it is an Australia "in which men and women fit comfortably into traditional gender roles" (2010, p. 68). As a celebrity whose presence within the campaign presents him as a representative of the nation, he further reinforces a national image that privileges whiteness and traditional, heteronormative gender roles. While the campaign re-characterizes Australia as a tranquil, natural and adventurous destination, it nonetheless conforms to pre-existing racialized (and gendered) discourses through its portrayal of Hemsworth.

Conclusion

A country's national identity is pivotal to tourism and people's general understanding of the culture. By examining Chris Hemsworth's celebrity status and the meaning transfer process, we are able to breakdown the key elements that craft his brand and how that can relate to Australia. His interview discussions about growing up in Australia with his brothers, further reinforces his attachment to his home country. Having global reach through his success playing Thor, means that utilizing his brand to sell the nation can reach a wider audience. Essentially, he holds celebrity capital that can be exploited to create economic capital for the country. However, while he helps to build Australia's identity, he also hinders it by reinforcing the notion of a white, blonde, attractive surfer identity. This chapter does not suggest that Hemsworth should not be an ambassador, but that other Australian celebrities that more accurately reflect the reality of Australia's Indigenous and multicultural society should be included. Additionally, a construction of Australian identity that does not rely on the masculine stereotype can be pursued.

References

Alomes, S. (1988). *A nation at last? The changing character of Australian nationalism* 1880-1988. NSW, North Ryde: Angus & Robertson.

Anderson, B. (2006). *Imagined communities reflections on the origin and spread of nationalism*. London: Verso Books.

Ang, l. (1999). Racial/spatial anxiety: 'Asia' in the psycho- geography of Australian whiteness. In G. Hage and R. Couche (Eds.) *The future of Australian multiculturalism* (pp. 189-204). NSW, Sydney: University of Sydney Press.

Australian Bureau of Statistics. (2016). *2024.0 - Census of population and housing: Australia revealed, 2016.* Retrieved January 5, 2018, from http://www.abs.gov.au/ausstats/abs@.nsf/Latestproducts/2024.0Main%20Features 22016?opendocument&tabname=Summary&prodno=2024.0&issue=2016&num= &view=

Baker, S.A., & Rowe, D. (2014). Mediating mega events and manufacturing multiculturalism: The cultural politics of the world game in Australia. *Journal of Sociology, 50*(3), 299–314.

BOSS. (2017). BOSS bottled: Man of today with Chris Hemsworth | HUGO BOSS Perfumes. *YouTube.* Retrieved December 14, 2017, from https://www.youtube.com/watch?v=wuolDtCniKc

CBAustralia. (2016). Chris Hemsworth stars in latest Foxtel 'Make It Yours' campaign via Whybin\TBWA. *YouTube.* Retrieved December 15, 2017, from https://www.youtube.com/watch?v=YFnM_vzsw1k

Chandler, D. (2017). *Semiotics for beginners.* Retrieved, January 16, 2018 from http://visual-memory.co.uk/daniel/Documents/S4B/sem06.html

CrossMediaOwnership. (2009). Paul Hogan Ad 1984. *YouTube.* Retrieved December 15, 2017, from https://www.youtube.com/watch?v=Xn_CPrCS8gs

Crotty, M. (2001). *Making the Australian male: Middle-class masculinity 1870-1920.* Victoria, Carlton South: Melbourne University Press.

Department of Immigration and Border Protection. (2015). *A history of the Department of Immigration: Managing migration to Australia.* Retrieved 11 January 11, 2017 from https://www.border.gov.au/CorporateInformation/Documents/immigration-history.pdf

Donoghue, J., & Tranter, B. (2015). The Anzacs: Military influences on Australian identity. *Journal of Sociology, 51*(3), 449–463.

Dyer, R. (1986). *Heavenly bodies.* London: BFI.

Feige, K. (Producer), & Branagh, K. (Director). (2011). *Thor* [Motion Picture]. United States: Marvel Studios.

Gamson, J. (1994). *Claims to fame: Celebrity in contemporary America.* California, Berkeley: University of California Press.

Gledhill, C. (1991). *Stardom: industry of desire.* London: Routledge.

Goulopoulos, S., & La Cioppa, B. (2016). 'It was never home': Chris Hemsworth opens up about moving back to Australia with his wife and children after living in L.A. *Daily Mail.* Retrieved December 10, 2017, from http://www.dailymail.co.uk/tvshowbiz/article-3432779/Chris-Hemsworth-admits-feels-immediate-affinity-home-Australia-returning-overseas.html

Hage, G. (1998). *White nation: Fantasies of white supremacy in a multicultural Society.* NSW, Sydney: Pluto Press.

Hage, G. (2002). Multiculturalism and white paranoia in Australia. *Journal of International Migration and Integration, 3*(3), 417-437.

Hogan, J. (2010). Gendered and racialised discourses of national identity in Baz Luhrmann's Australia. *Journal of Australian Studies,* 34 (1), 63-77.

Holmes, S., & and Redmond, S. (2012). *Framing celebrity: New directions in celebrity culture.* Hoboken: Taylor and Francis.

Howard, R. (Director). (2013). *Rush* [Motion Picture]. USA: Exclusive Media Group.

IMDb. (2017). *Chris Hemsworth.* Retrieved January 16, 2018, from http://www.imdb.com/name/nm1165110/

Ironside, R. (2016). Chris Hemsworth's sexy voice is luring tourists Down Under. *News.com.* Retrieved December 13, 2017, from http://www.news.com.au/travel/travel-updates/chris-hemsworths-sexy-voice-is-luring-tourists-down-under/news-story/2e115f0ba061c765581ae1d9607b7bc5

Katzin, L.H. (Director). (1971). *Le Mans* [Motion Picture]. USA: Cinema Center Films.

Luhrmann, B., & Knapman, C. (Producers), & Luhrmann, B. (Director). (2008). *Australia* [Motion Picture]. Australia: Bazmark Films.

Marshall, P.D. (2010). The promotion and presentation of the self: celebrity as marker of presentational media. *Celebrity Studies,* 1 (1), 35–48.

Marshall, P.D. (2016). *The celebrity persona pandemic.* Minneapolis: University of Minnesota Press.

McCracken, G. (2011). Who is the celebrity endorser? Cultural foundations of the endorsement process. *Chicago Journals, 16* (3), 310-321.

Moran, L. (2016). Constructions of race: symbolic ethnic capital and the performance of youth identity in multicultural Australia. *Ethnic and Racial Studies, 39*(4), 708-726.

MoviemaniacsDE. (2016). Thor Ragnarok - Thor on vacation during Captain America 3. *YouTube.* Retrieved December 14, 2017, from https://www.youtube.com/watch?v=K5PYZR30sG4

O'Shaughnessy, M., & Stadler, J. (2012). *Media and Society* (5th ed.)*.* Victoria, Melbourne: Oxford University Press.

Screen Australia. (2016). *Seeing ourselves: Reflections on diversity in Australian TV drama.* Retrieved January 5, 2018, from https://www.screenaustralia.gov.au/getmedia/157b05b4-255a-47b4-bd8b-9f715555fb44/TV-Drama-Diversity.pdf

Team Coco. (2012). Liam Hemsworth and his brothers fought with fists & knives - CONAN on TBS. *YouTube*. Retrieved January 16, 2018 from https://www.youtube.com/watch?v=Zp9z05zruWU

Thompson. K. (2007). The Australian larrikin: C. J. Dennis's [Un]sentimental Bloke. *Antipodies, 2007 (Dec), 177-183.*

Tourism Australia. (2016). *Chris Hemsworth announced as Tourism Australia's new global ambassador.* Retrieved December 15, 2017, from http://www.tourism.australia.com/news/media-releases-17747.aspx

Tranter, B., & Donoghue, J. (2008). Bushrangers Ned Kelly and Australian identity. *Journal of Sociology*, *44*(4), 373-390.

Wigney, J. (2017). Chris Hemsworth talks brotherly bust-ups, shooting at Liam and finding the lighter side of Thor. *News.com*. Retrieved December 17, 2017, from http://www.news.com.au/entertainment/movies/new-movies/chris-hemsworth-talks-brotherly-bustups-shooting-at-liam-and-finding-the-lighter-side-of-thor/news-story/3d6ba8edb6c206e7e6aecfe280e9e952

Waititi, T. (Director). (2017). *Thor: Ragnarok* [Motion Picture]. USA: Marvel Studios.

Generation Z: Visual Self-Governance through Photography

Kerstin Hacker

Abstract. Zambia is presented to the West through prevailing visual narratives of Africa's population growth, epidemics and poverty. This continual overexposure to similar images creates a familiarity with a visual narrative which is rarely questioned and often feeds into a narrative of 'Afro-pessimism'. Everyday life, however, as experienced by Zambia's growing affluent middle class in its urban centers, could not be further from these preconceived images. I have been photographing the series Generation Z in Zambia's capital Lusaka since 2016, and am documenting the rapidly developing city. This chapter explores the photographic series for its representational function, as well as its engagement with extant theoretical perspectives on Africa. It is critical that new photographic work contributes to the displacement of stereotypes and encourages viewers to contemplate the development processes of a country. Many post-colonial countries were, until now, denied access to photographic education, their own visual history and research into visual self-governance. However, this lack of research about photographic image production in Zambia in itself does not mean that there is no image production. In my series Generation Z, I attempt to combine the acknowledgement of my own Western visual heritage with the experience of extended stays in Lusaka. I ask viewers to contemplate change in Zambia and dismantle neocolonial visual discourses. I contend that it is important not to return to the limited visual research material available, and to not use outdated reference material from the 'colonial libraries', as that in itself would not acknowledge the 'uncited' recent developments.

Keywords: Visual Self-Governance, photography, practice research, Zambia, representation, colonial library

Introduction

Zambia, officially the Republic of Zambia, is a landlocked country in Southern Africa, neighboring the Democratic Republic of Congo to the north, Tanzania to the north-east, Malawi to the east, Mozambique, Zimbabwe, Botswana and Namibia to the south, and Angola to the west. It has a peaceful and democratic recent history and its economic fortunes depend on commodity prices like copper. As a country, it has stayed largely under the radar of international news agencies.

According to Scott Martin (2017), only one study was conducted on the representation of Zambia in the media between 1950 and 2012. In his research, Martin looks at the wider representation of Africa in the media, and argues that "existing research into US and UK representations of Africa [have] a remarkably narrow focus on a specific number of countries, events, media and texts" (p. 203). He further argues that apart from the representation of key events such as the 1994 Rwanda genocide or the collapse of the Apartheid system, "we know almost nothing about how the majority of the continent is covered by most US and UK media, most of the time" (p. 203).

Because of the limited visual material available about Zambia, the country is perceived by Western audiences through prevailing narratives of Africa through images of population growth, epidemics and poverty; however, everyday life, as experienced by Zambia's growing affluent middle class in its urban centers, could not be further from these preconceived images. These factors make Zambia a key location in which to explore the idea of Visual Self-Governance in low income countries.

The term of self-governance in an African context describes an emancipation of local and national politics, trying to shed postcolonial and resist neocolonial governance structures, which have their roots in colonial rule. These governmental structures remain embedded within the newly formed nations. In most African countries, independence did not lead to a restructuring of local and national governance and therefore the newly established governments largely reproduce 'things', in a Foucauldian sense. Foucault (1978) suggests that "what government has to do with is not territory but, rather, a sort of complex composed of men and things" (p. 208). In his essay on *Governmentality* he states:

> The things, in a sense, with which government is to be concerned are in fact men, but men in their relations, their links, their imbrications with those things that are wealth, resources, means of subsistence, the territory with its specific qualities, climate, irrigation, fertility, and so on; men in their relation to those other things that are customs, habits, ways of acting and thinking and so on; and finally men in relation to those still other things that might be accidents and misfortunes such as famine, epidemics, death and so on. (p. 208)

I argue that *visual self-governance* can study representations of relationships between men and things and can eloquently question legacy power structures that have stayed static in post-colonial Africa. Visual self-governance contributes clearly to how relations between men and things, and therefore governments, are understood both by its citizens and outside observers. Currently much visual material depicting low income countries evokes colonial narratives relating to *things* from the past. Nevertheless, the visual arts have the capacity to contradict or reject colonial, post-colonial and neo-colonial narratives and artistic practices are often influenced by local and national narratives. The visual relationship of people in low income countries and *things* have until now often been depicted by non-domestic media. The ability for citizens to define and challenge these relationships through self-governing the image will allow for a representation of the self, and will also influence how audiences see the nation.

It is therefore important for artists to be involved in the development of self-governance both by creating new imagery exploring the relationship between men and 'non-colonial' *things*, but also re-contextualizing historic material. Visual self-governance allows practitioners and audiences to break with static narratives and allows for new cultural realities to evolve.

As a practicing artist/photographer and researcher I juxtapose practice with theory and theory with practice, as theory emerges from a reflexive practice at the same time as practice is informed by theory. This research process can be complex in nature. It is a generative enquiry that draws on interdisciplinary and emergent methodologies which have the potential to extend definitions on how new knowledge is produced.

I have been photographing the series *Generation Z* in Lusaka, the capital of Zambia, since 2016, and am documenting modern life in the rapidly developing city. The series documents the experience of a new wealthy section of society by photographing environments such as shopping centers (Fig. 1), ballet classes (Fig. 2) and family gatherings.

To a Western audience, the images look strangely familiar, as if they might have been photographed in one of the urban centers in the United Kingdom or United States. The images, at first glance, are street photographs, and refer to known canons of visual references, both historical and contemporary. However, upon further investigation, the images provide hints as to where they have been taken: the fast food chains are not familiar; the light is glaring; and even the street furniture is markedly different. It becomes clear that these images have been produced in Africa. It is at this point that the apparently ordinary becomes unfamiliar, and doesn't meet expectations of the viewer.

Fig. 1. Supermarket in Lusaka - From the photographic series Generation Z (original in color).

Fig. 2. Ballet Class - From the photographic series Generation Z (original in color).

My photographic work should not be regarded as illustrations complementing the theoretical text, but rather explore how the process of making will challenge more traditional notions of research. My practice seeks eloquence in its own right and reveals insights that are only possible through artistic and photographic process. The process values intuition and experience, which I draw upon during the making of these images. The photographs themselves hereby propose a discourse and exploration with the theoretical research material in this chapter.

Uncited Visual Narratives

The Congolese philosopher Valentin-Yves Mudimbe argued in his seminal book *The Invention of Africa: Gnosis, Philosophy and the Order of Knowledge* (1988), that audiences often take their references from a narrow pool of narratives, which cite existing references from a "colonial library" (p. 195). This concept of the colonial library can also be transferred to the visual and refers to images of poverty, under-development, disease, and black people who are generally represented as voiceless.

We can find a similar observation again nearly thirty years later when Columbia University professor Howard W. French, a veteran *New York Times* correspondent and expert for West and Central Africa, bemoans this anachronistic style of coverage in modern American journalism on the subject of Africa. In 2015, he wrote to the CBS News flagship program *60 Minutes*, to express his concerns about their coverage: "Africans are limited to the role of passive victims, or occasionally brutal and corrupt villains and incompetents; they are not otherwise shown to have any agency or even the normal range of human thoughts and emotions" (French, 2015). It can be argued that this representation of Africa is deliberately nourished by stories that tap into colonial history, often simplistically playing off white against black, rich against poor, the powerful against the powerless and the people with a voice against the voiceless. These juxtapositions make for easy story writing, sit comfortably within the canon of post-colonial narratives and are simple to produce and sell.

This form of narrative will persist as long as viewers do not accept that realities are much more nuanced than the Western media wants us to believe, and as long Africa does not produce images and stories themselves. As Homi Bhabha suggests, as long as "one silence uncannily repeats the other, the sign of identity and reality found in the work of the empire is slowly undone" (1994, p. 124). Similarly, Guido Rings (2016) argues in *Otherness in Contemporary European Cinema* that news coverage of Africa is no coincidence but stems from historic and colonial narratives, which are deliberately evoked again and again:

> On a representational level, this implies the continuity of binary constructs within which former colonizers and succeeding national elites tend to portray themselves to formally colonized or neo-colonized 'Others' as rational, civilized, and male representatives of a superior order, which leaves more instinctive, barbarian, and female roles for the Others. (p. 14)

There *is* a growing interest in a more emancipated visual self-representation of the African continent in mainstream media like the Marvel film *Black Panther* (2018), which features an heroic, all-black cast in a fictional African country. Other examples include photographers Pieter Hugo and Zanele Muholi, who explore their South African heritage and identity through their work and have been invited into the Western art scene as representatives of the continent. Despite these instances of cultural engagement with the African continent, it seems that the discourses that sparked Mudimbe's definition of the 'colonial library' persist. One could therefore state that this continual overexposure to similar images creates a familiarity with a visual narrative which is not questioned, but rather remains static, often feeding into a narrative of 'Afro-pessimism'. Afro-pessimism refers to the influence these visual narratives still have on the whole African continent and how power structures are shaped through preexisting narratives of the continent. Many Zambian artists and photographers are painfully aware of the discrepancy between the stories they need to tell, and those which are told about them.

A quest for visual self-governance and more current representation is not unique to Zambia or the African continent. We have witnessed subtle and steady changes in perception of countries such as South Korea, Jamaica or even Australia over the years. At the beginning of the 21st century India also began the debate on how to take control of the internal and external representation and Indian media houses took an active part in changing perceptions. In 2005, picture editor Bandeep Singh from India's largest news magazine *India Today* made the point that their magazine chose to no longer visually emphasize the depiction of poverty but showcase a more diverse India and therefore allow a debate on self-representation and visual self-governance of the nation (B. Singh, personal communication, February 10, 2018).

Zambia might be at a similar point now where it is ready to reevaluate its image. It will be important to document how far and how fast views on Zambia shift when Zambian or other African photographers take over. We will see the deconstruction of Western ideologies like Afro-pessimism only when nations recognize the importance of their own visual representation.

From the time of its invention, photography has been used to support guided ideologies about people and countries. The medium lends itself to documenting faraway, foreign places, which many people might never otherwise have the chance to see for themselves. Such images rely upon the interpretation of the traveling photographers. All too often, with specific markets in mind, photographers seek out what an audience is already familiar with and feeds existing expectations and assumptions. Therefore, established narratives can take a long time to shift.

Documentary photography, in its heyday, was predicated on a principle that the photographer's nationality did not matter. As Susan Sontag describes, in *Regarding the Pain of Other*s: "The photographer's nationality and national journalistic affiliation were, in principle, irrelevant." (2004, p. 31) Historically, it was important what they were willing to endure and where they were willing to go. Photographers made their living by being closely connected to established media markets, and by building networks with editors and publishers. However, the profession has been racially skewed (and previously gender specific). The celebrated photographic agency Magnum was founded in 1947 by a group of white European men, manifesting a bias towards images produced through a Western-centric lens. This is still largely true today. Photographers from the African continent only represent a tiny number of photographers whose work is published and recognized. In 2017, the *World Press Photo Awards*, one of the most recognized industry awards, received 80,408 images from 5034 photographers (World Press Photo Contest Technical Report, 2017, p. 2). Of these, only two percent were from African photographers and only one African photographer was amongst the prize winners. Even in 2014, at the height of the Ebola Crisis in West Africa, there was only one African photographer awarded (2017, p. 11). Nevertheless, most of the images in the competition come from what Susan Sontag describes as "memorable sites of suffering" in Asia and Africa (2004, p.33)

It is this lack of control over a nation's own image and its depiction in the media outlets which highlights where the power over the image lies. Power lies not with individual photographers, but the national and private cultural institutions that the photographer operates within. These cultural institutions need to actively work towards a broader representation and need to recognize the importance of visual self-governance, rather than relying on the 'colonial library' as a reference.

Furthermore, it becomes now apparent that, as Andrea Ballatore, Mark Graham and Shilad Sen suggest, "a few countries in the Global North play an inordinately large role in defining the digital augmentations of the Global South" (2017, p. 19). A search for 'Zambia Photo' on the Yahoo site reveals a narrow set of images: African wild life, simple food and images of poor children in rural areas. Google produced a similar set of images, with a greater focus on Western tourists observing landscapes and wildlife. There is no recognizable imagery that might be considered as unique to Zambia. In this regard, Google images of Zambia aligns with the wider visual narrative of Africa – its bush landscapes and wild life – with which Western audiences are familiar. According to Ballatore, Graham and Sen (2017), content about the geographic South is mostly produced in the geographic North, because:

> ...since the company's creation in 1998, Google's algorithms have tended to favor highly central Web content: Pages linked to by a lot of other pages are prioritized, and those largely ignored are demoted in the rankings. This creates a worrying situation whereby it becomes difficult for those on the information peripheries to break out of their digital marginality (p.19)

It is this digital marginality – and questions around its intentionality or existence as a byproduct of the digitization of knowledge – that re-emphasizes that there are degrees of access to knowledge. Even with the existence of technical capabilities to provide access to all knowledge to all humans, this knowledge is filtered. For our own convenience, we accept this filtering, often without considering the discourses it is replicating. Research is only just beginning on who does not have access to the information and how this impacts on knowledge creation. As digital content in countries like the UK and US grows exponentially, the margins of the world wide web are still broadly unexposed.

In *The Cited and the Uncited: Towards an Emancipatory Reading of Representations of Africa* Garuba and Himmelman (2012) argue that Edward Said's definition of Orientalism, as "a system for citing texts and authors" (Said cited in Garuba & Himmelman, 2012, p. 23), also plays out in the visual culture by quoting the 'colonial library'. Images which do not quote from the colonial library could be envisioned as a step towards an emancipatory reading of representations of Africa (p.17), and are referred to as 'uncited' by Garuba and Himmelman. The 'uncited' can be conceptualized as a "blank, uninscribed space, that is still outside of discursive representation" (2012, p. 17). The question then arises; whether these blank, uninscribed places, are being willfully left blank, or if ignorance is a valid excuse for an unwillingness to engage?

It is critical that new work fills some of these blank spaces and starts to displace the visual cultural and political myths that have become entrenched, and asks viewers to contemplate the development processes of a country. In my work, I am concentrating on the urban narrative, which is currently underrepresented, and therefore can offer an additional interpretation of the contemporary African experience.

Samantha Wehbi and Deane Taylor (2012) argue that:

> Holding on to an awareness of our potential to reproduce problematic North/South power relations, and taking on the responsibility of anti-colonial resistance, we have the possibility of producing alternative images that involve creating representations that reflect the attempts of people from the North and South to work together in solidarity to resist the dominant neocolonial discourses of our time. (p. 537)

Therefore, documenting the modern urban life in Lusaka questions what development means for African cities. It juxtaposes the celebration of ambition and consumerism of middle class Africa with the concern that the continent will assimilate to neoliberal ideals. One could argue that the remaining 'otherness' of Africa gives the continent a distinct and unique character and that an assimilation to Western ideals will create sustainability issues the West is all too familiar with.

Visual Self-Governance through Photography

In collaboration with the Mass Communication department at the University of Zambia, which began in 2009, we developed an under graduate curriculum for photography to foster visual self-governance. The curriculum addresses the need to heighten visual literacy amongst the student populace and supports them to find their own voice. The collaboration brought together the structure of a well-established Western photography course with the need of a de-colonialized, country specific curriculum.

In my series *Generation Z*, I attempt to combine the acknowledgement of my own Western visual heritage with the experience of extended stays in Lusaka. I ask viewers to contemplate change in Zambia and dismantle neocolonial visual discourses. There is a real interest in Zambia to see an alternative representation of the country. The interest was for images less laden with colonial and post-colonial references; images that were shaking off the burden of representation, and which were less attached to a post-colonial narrative.

In August 2017, the *Generation Z* series was exhibited at the Henry Tayali Gallery in Zambia, by invitation of the Visual Arts Council of Zambia. The *Generation Z* series was originally aimed at a Western audience, however, it also sparked debate amongst Zambian photographers on how to develop methods of showing a wider, more diverse view of their country, which highlights its unique character. The discussions highlighted that Zambia's visual identity outside the country, and to some extent within the country, is often based on a stereotypical African narrative, which was felt not to reflect life experienced within Zambia. It is therefore not a question of if my photographs are the 'correct' representation of modern Africa, but if they contribute to the debate on how Zambia could be represented. These images sparked a debate on the dangers of neo-liberal consumerism on African culture and what this means to the people of Zambia, but also illustrated the visual 'proof' of the so often demanded economic progress of an African nation. It highlights the chasm between Zambians' daily experience of their urban lives in Lusaka, and the photographs they see of themselves in the international media.

Through my previous work with the University of Zambia and the Visual Arts Council, I was also asked to run a two-week workshop parallel with the exhibition with a group of photographers with a range of different backgrounds. The participants were commercial photographers, fine artists, photojournalists and a filmmaker. In the workshop, we developed a dialogue about how Zambia could be represented, and how photographers can contribute to the development of a visual narrative of a nation that will allow them to work toward visual self- governance. Gerald Mwale, photojournalism lecturer at the University of Zambia, observed that "photography is, in fact, a way to better understand one's surroundings" (2017). We therefore discussed the current visual post-colonial representation of Africa and specifically Zambia and developed strategies on how to heighten the awareness of the continuous reference to the 'colonial library'.

By revisiting the historic and current theoretical texts as part of my research, I established that there is a long-standing awareness for the need of a more diverse representation of Africa, but also a distinct lack of action to address the problem. In Zambia, poor access to research materials, the lack of engagement by the Zambian academic community and the absence of funding for research into visual representation can be cited as the key factors that limit local research.

This, combined with disinterest from more established research centers in the West, created a vacuum that allowed the status quo to fester for many decades. If this non-engagement with the questions about the representation of Africa is a deliberate act to keep power structures in place also needs further investigation.

In my photographic practice, I reacted intuitively to these issues. Working both in practice and theory allows me to explore these theoretical concepts, visualizing some of the more challenging questions laid out in this chapter. My photographs document the everyday, the unsensational and often unnoticed moments of societal change in Lusaka. The nature of photography, the recording of split seconds of time, allows the recognition that change has occurred.

Zambian artists and photographers in the workshop discussions were unsure if the simple everyday is worthwhile recording, and if these everyday activities warranted a large-scale exhibition. They questioned the purpose of recording the ordinary, as the ordinary was kept private for many decades, not worth discussing within the established theoretical framework of self-representation. Zambia had been, until now, only represented by the extraordinary, the wild life, waterfalls and various stereotypical depictions of the poor, which most Zambians do not recognize as a true depiction of their country. It is the contradiction of the ordinary that is *uncited* and the extraordinary that is *cited*, that is discussed in my practical work.

Fig. 3. Street Scene - From the photographic series Generation Z (original in color).

Concluding remarks

Further research on if and how the established theoretical framework can contribute to the debate of visual self-governance in Zambia, and if this framework is fit for purpose, still needs to be conducted. At the moment, most research on visual representation is about low income countries rather than engaging in a meaningful dialogue with the countries. I contend that, because of the lack of information, it is important for researchers like myself not to return to the limited research material available, and to not use outdated reference material from the 'colonial libraries', as that in itself would not acknowledge the 'uncited' visual practices which happened over the last sixty years.

Speaking at the event *Who do you think you are? Culture, identity and the contemporary art museum* (2017), Nigerian art critic Okwui Enwezor, curator of the 2015, highlighted the responsibility galleries have to national audiences. As cultural institutions galleries, need to take responsibility for decolonizing art production in their countries. There is therefore a need to invest in national photographic institutions, which are able to build the foundations for a discourse about Zambia's media image, and develop new approaches which do not make the colonial past the central argument, but invest in its own visual history; and build national archives from disperse collections that are degrading or getting lost as time passes. It is therefore urgent to do this archival research work now, and to ensure a visually literate and critical workforce is fostered to preserve these invaluable and historic documents.

Toussaint Nothias (2014) argues that, if no effort is made, the danger is that this blank space will be filled by generic imagery of neither historic nor cultural relevance to the country. It is therefore important that African nations find their own visual narrative as otherwise "African identities and the continent's future are visualized in the increasingly homogenized and generic visual language of global neoliberalism" (p. 336).

In a time where we are flooded with images and it is said that photography is no longer needed as everything has been photographed already, it is important to understand that these statements come from a privileged, but limited Western perspective. This perspective does not take into account the fact that many post-colonial countries were, until now, denied access to photographic education, their own visual history and the research into visual self-governance. As this research still has to be done, we still might find other icons of African photography, similar to Seydou Keita or Malick Sidibe in Mali.

This chapter suggests that much more will need to be done to understand and support the ways in which Zambia, and Africa in general, visually represents its own communities and countries. It highlights factors that constrained this development until now. I hope that this chapter will be useful to the photographic and academic community of Zambia as they foster self-representation and visual self-governance of their nation.

Acknowledgments

I am grateful to Anglia Ruskin University for granting a sabbatical, which allowed me to spend a prolonged time photographing and researching in Zambia. I would like to thank Gerald Mwale, Lecturer in Mass Communication at University of Zambia, the Visual Arts Council of Zambia and Zambian artist Geoffrey Phiri for helping me understand and contextualize what was in front of me. I would also like to thank Jenni Skinner, librarian at the Centre for African Studies at the University of Cambridge, who opened up a whole raft of research materials and made me feel at home at the library.

References

Anon (2017). *The 2017 world press photo contest technical report*. Retrieved October 19, 2017, from https://www.worldpressphoto.org/sites/default/files/upload/2017_wppftechnnicalreport.pdf.

Ballatore, A., Graham, M & Sen, S. (2017): Digital hegemonies: The localness of search engine results. *Annals of the American association of geographers*, DOI: 10.1080/24694452.2017.1308240.

Bhabha, H.K. (1994). *The location of culture*. London: Routledge.

Foucault, M. (2000[1978]) Governmentality. In Faubion, J. (Ed.) *Power: Michel Foucault essential works of Foucault 1954-1984 volume 3* (pp. 201-222). London: Penguin Books.

French, H. (2015, March 25). *How does Africa get reported? A letter of concern to 60 Minutes*. Retrieved, November 1, 2017, from http://www.howardwfrench.com/2015/03/how-does-africa-get-reported-a-letter-of-concern-to-60-minutes/.

Feige, K. (Producer), & Coogle, R. (Director) (2018) *Black Panther* [Motion Picture]. United States of America: Walt Disney Studios Motion Pictures.

Garuba, H. & Himmleman, N. (2012). The cited and the uncited: Towards an emancipatory reading of representations of Africa. In Higgins, M.E. (Ed.). *Hollywood's Africa after 1994* (pp. 15-34). Athens: Ohio University Press.

Hacker, K (2017, February 14). *Generation Z*. Retrieved, December 17, 2017, from www.kerstinhacker.org/zambia

Mudimbé, V. Y. (1988) *The invention of Africa: Gnosis, philosophy, and the order of knowledge*. Bloomington: Indiana University Press.

Mwale, G. (2017) The need for professional photography in Zambia. In Hacker, K. (Ed.) *Generation Z* (p. 7). Cambridge: Self-published

Nothias, T. (2013). 'Rising', 'hopeful', 'new': visualizing Africa in the age of globalization. *Visual Communication 13(3)* 323-339. DOI 10.1177/1470357214530063

Rings, G. (2016). *Otherness in contemporary European cinema*. New York: Routledge

Said, E., (1997 [1978]). *Orientalism*. New York: Vintage

Scott, M. (2017). The myth of representations of Africa: A comprehensive scoping review of the literature. *Journalism Studies* [e-journal] 18(2) http://www.tandfonline.com/doi/full/10.1080/1461670X.2015.1044557

Sontag, S. (2004). *Regarding the pain of others.* London: Penguin

This is Tomorrow, (2017, March 19). Stuart Hall Foundation, *Who do you think you are? Culture, identity and the contemporary art museum*. Retrieved, December 17, 2017, from https://www.youtube.com/watch?v=EY9sI1GKu2A&t=2397s

Wehbi, S. &Taylor, D. (2012). Photographs speak louder than words: the language of international development images. *Community Development Journal*, 48, 525 – 539

Part II:
Representing People and Society

Alternative Australia: (Re)constructing 'normality' through Australian celebrities

Louise St Guillaume, Ellen Finlay and Celia Lam

Abstract. Contemporary Australian society is fostered upon settler colonial race relations and multicultural immigration policies that encourages the co-existence of different cultures within a broader, civic, notion of an Australian identity. This Australian identity is adopted in internal discourse to reinforce 'positive' societal values and condemn 'negative' values through the lens of 'Australian/un-Australian'. However, a definition of Australian identity within a settler colonial, multicultural state is often ambiguous. Indeed, the 'face' of Australia – those personal (or physical) characteristics that define individuals as 'Australian' – is increasingly contested in Australian society. Despite this, Australian media representation is, for the most part, homogenous. Recent reports, including a report from the Government funded Screen Australia (2016), highlights Australian media's lack of diverse representation. This chapter examines three Australian celebrities who differ from the Euro-centric, male, able-bodied model that dominates Australian media. It examines their place within the Australian media-scape for their ability to at once challenge and reinforce the dominant image. While their presence would appear to contest a 'white-washed' representation of Australian national identity, the presentation of their public personas is as much shaped and confined by the dominant image as it opposes it. In particular, activities associated with advocacy and activism is foregrounded only after a primary persona (generally professional or niche) is firmly established.

Keywords: Stan Grant, Adam Hills, Dami Im, Australian national identity, Celebrity.

Introduction

Contemporary Australian national identity is constructed based on racialized social and immigration policies that, until very recently, have been exclusionary in nature. Australia is a settler-colonial state with a documented history of invasion, dispossession and destruction of Indigenous peoples. Australia originally excluded Indigenous peoples from being counted as part of the nation. It was not until the 1967 Referendum when Indigenous peoples were counted in the national census (Thomas, 2017). Furthermore, colonizers inflicting harm on Indigenous peoples, particularly during frontier violence were rarely prosecuted – the exception being the Myall Creek Massacre in 1838 where settlers were hanged for massacring Wirrayaraay people. This event is an anomaly in Australian history because the law was upheld against the white settlers at a time when the killing of Indigenous peoples was otherwise normalized in the process of dispossession and invasion (Australia Government Department of Environment and Energy, n.d.; Korff, 2017). Upon Federation in 1901 Australia enacted the Immigration Restriction Act 1901 (also known as the White Australia policy), which restricted the migration of non-white individuals and those assessed to be physically and/or cognitively impaired (Soldatic & Fiske, 2009). Furthermore, though Australia was one of the first countries in the world to give women the right to vote, women have been underrepresented in Australian parliaments (McCann & Wilson, 2014) and femininity derided in Australian culture (Bird, 1983). These policies and values constitute a restrictive national identity, which is normalized through discourse and media.

The 'normal' is a powerful discursive tool, which (following Foucault) is strategically applied to define and exclude, to shape and structure and to limit human subjectivity within a society. It is both conceptually and materially present within a semiotic system, and most prevalent in contemporary culture and media discourses. Within an Australian context, normalized identities are racialized, gendered and often grounded within ableist discourses, such that deviation from a 'white', 'male' and 'able bodied' identity is felt to require justification. Thus, the (media) constructions and (self) identity performed by Australian celebrities are defined by broader notions of the 'normal', which construct and delimit, or 'govern', the individual celebrity.

The analysis of Australian celebrities Stan Grant, Adam Hills and Dami Im in this chapter seeks to critique notions of the 'normal' by examining the discursive construction and ongoing performance of their public (and private) personas. From different perspectives these three case studies reinforce a normalized identity within Australia, governed by the construction of a dominant 'national identity' that restricts their individual capacity to present alternative representations of Australian identity. This chapter problematizes the national stories produced through the media as "a key space where knowledge, including national stories, ... [are] produced" (Elder, Pratt & Ellis, 2006, p. 183) and examines the identities of these three celebrities to critique how the notion of 'normal' is featured in media and cultural discourses within the Australian context. This chapter will outline how normalized identities are defined within the Australian context, articulated through a framework of 'normality', which is both constructed by the media and performed by the celebrities. Data supporting this chapter is sourced, using a purposive sampling technique, from media reports, media appearances and publications written by the celebrities in question.

Literature Review

Associated with national identity is nationalism, which functions "not to define Australia as a real entity but to represent Australia as an ideological construction" (Johanson & Glow, 2009, p. 386). This ideological construction is a project by which the boundaries of a national culture are defined through drawing on symbolism and myth-making, producing meaning through presentation and representation. Australian national identity is built upon the mythology of what constitutes a 'true' representation of the Australian nation. Australia has gravitated towards celebrating idealized notions of masculinity, whiteness and ableism, which embody physicality, strength, stoicism, heroism, hard work, 'egalitarianism', a 'fair-go' and disregard for authority. Figures such as, the bushman, the ANZAC and the bronzed 'beach going' Aussie constitute this mythology, alongside Australia's obsession with sport (Gardiner, 2003; Goggin & Newell, 2005; Smith & Phillips, 2006). These cherished values shape the construction of the nation, how Australia understands itself and how it represents itself in the media. As mentioned, this representation is predominately Anglo-European in nature. As Elder et al. suggests, in "Australia the production of ideas of national belonging has centralized the experiences of white Australians and marginalized Indigenous belonging through the historical processes of dispossession, eradication and assimilation" (2006, p. 185).[1] Similarly, the national narrative excludes the histories of migration and disability, producing "an 'imaginary unity'" through the imposition of "model[s] of identity/difference" (Shapiro, 1999, p. 48 cited in Elder et al., 2006, p. 185). Unity is thus, reinforced not through inclusion but through exclusion.

Johanson and Glow suggest there are numerous "[a]rguments [in scholarship] that historically, Australian nationalism has been underpinned by patriarchal, capitalist and racist values" (2009, p. 386). Scholars in disability studies have highlighted that the Australian identity is premised on the hegemony of the able-body. Ann Curthoys (2009) argues Australia has made whiteness in the national identity invisible as a means of obscuring the violence against Indigenous Australians and the exclusion of migrants labelled "alien races" (p. 9). To Marilyn Lake (1997) androcentrism in the dominant national narratives of Australian public discourses silences the contribution of women; "their significance was ignored in national stories of the making of the nation"

---

[1] It is important to acknowledge that "[a]lthough contemporary Australian nationalism is still a predominantly white project, it now depends on signifiers of Indigeneity [...as] Indigenous symbols have been appropriated and integrated into Australian nationalist discourse" (Elder, et.al., 2006: 186).

(p. 48). Other writers have explained that Australia used national immigration policy as a way to shape the national identity, which allowed a public to imagine "a community united by particular values" (Johanson and Glow, 2009, p. 386).

It can be argued that the 'mainstream' media perform an important role in constructing and disseminating the idealized image of the Australian nation and its values as the media plays a significant role in nation building (Smith & Phillips, 2006). Furthermore, the genre of media that people engage with shapes their acceptance of national boundary maintenance or permeability and an inclusive or exclusive national identity (Smith & Phillips, 2006). The media thus, has a role in shaping people's understanding of the world and their position within it. Research on media effects is contested terrain (Hall, 1980; McRobbie, 2005; Morley, 1992). Yet scholars have documented the impact of the media on identity construction. Exclusionary narratives produced via media also impact on people's sense of belonging to the nation state. For instance, Akbarzadeh (2016) discusses how Islamophobia has contributed to the alienation of Muslim youth in Australian society.

The Australian media has been critiqued for its representation of 'normal' Australia, perpetuating a white, able-bodied, masculine narrative. From an Indigenous lens Meadows (1995; Meadows & Morris, 1998) suggests that Indigenous peoples are often misrepresented in the media in order to frame "Indigenous peoples in particular ways" (Meadows, 2004, p. 281). Images or stories reflecting Indigenous peoples often depict violence, deviance, criminality, abuse, anarchy, hopelessness, dependency and alcoholism. These representations play into already entrenched stereotypes (Atherford, 2006; Gargett, 2005; Hollinsworth, 2005; Langton, 2008; Meadows, 1995; Watson, 1978), which become further embedded as they are extensively "repeated and reinforced" (Weston, 1996, p. 2 cited in Meadows, 2004, p. 276). Hollinsworth suggests that "in the case of Indigenous Australians, the problem is not ... underrepresentation ... [but] ... representation within pathologised and racist frameworks" (2005, p. 17). Meadows comparatively argues that the misrepresentations about Indigenous peoples that are pervasive in the media have "helped enshrine racism at an institutional level in Australia" (1995, p. 18). The mainstream media's unchallenging representation of Indigenous peoples often compounds misrepresentation based on stereotypes but also distorts the voices of Indigenous peoples and Indigenous media products that disrupt and interrogate the motifs and productions of the mainstream media (Hollinsworth, 2005). In addition, the control of the media, which generally resides in the hands of the non-Indigenous majority, raises concerns for the representations of Indigenous peoples and their inclusion within representations of national identity.

Similarly, in relation to disability, Goggin and Newell (2005, p. 116) argue that the media does not provide diverse representations of people with disability, often perpetuating representations of disability as a tragedy and a catastrophe. People with disability have also been represented as violent (Henderson, 2017; Rowe, Tilbury, Rapley & Ferrall, 2003) and portrayed to invoke charity, sympathy and pity. This means that the complexity of the lived experience of disability is obscured in favor of problematic representations. The media also excludes the voices of people with disability from media representations (Goggin & Newell, 2005, p. 209). Goggin and Newell suggest that "[w]e need to analyse and contest the mainstream media's construction of disability" (2005, p. 117) and provide a platform for the voices of people with disability to be included in media representations.

Furthermore, representations of the idealized Australian tends to replicate the masculinized, White, image of figures such as the bushman, the ANZAC and the bronzed beach lover. Discussing Baz Lurhmann's 2008 film *Australia*, Jackie Hogan suggests its adherence to a set of narratives that create Australian national identity through "fetishising white Australian manhood and marginalizing women and non-white Others" (2010, p. 63). This results in the sidelining of exceptions – non-white, non-male individuals – in the national imagination (Hogan, 2010). Similarly, Lake highlights the under emphasis of women, suggesting that despite their role in Australian life and culture, "women were nevertheless, rendered invisible as national subjects" (1997, p.47). The image of an 'Australian' is thus, constructed in the media as predominately male, white and able-bodied. This image, and the national narrative in which it is embedded, becomes the basis from which belonging is determined. Deviation from this image is often felt to require justification, in order to establish a connection to the existing national identity. This chapter seeks to map the complexity of how the Australian celebrity case studies interact with the image of 'normal' Australia. It highlights how the celebrities embrace, challenge, or subvert the image in their private and public personas.

Framework – a model of 'normality'

In order to examine the celebrities and their relationship to the 'normalized' Australian identity, this chapter will explore the interaction of the celebrities with centralized identifiers of a 'normal' Australian identity. These identifiers are evident within the myth of the white, able-bodied male 'typical' Australian in different ways. As Figure 1 (below) shows, and as will be explained, all interact with these central characteristics but seek to extend or embed themselves in the 'norm' in different ways.

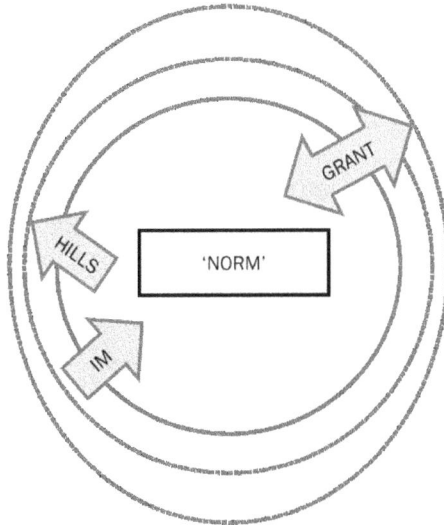

Fig. 1. Grant, Hills and Im mapped to spheres of 'normality'.

Case Studies

Stan Grant

Stan Grant is a Wiradjuri elder whose career as a broadcaster and journalist has spanned 30 years. He has won numerous awards, including a Walkey (for excellence in journalism) for his 2016 memoir *Talking to my Country*. He has also held various roles in commercial and public television and worked overseas as an international broadcaster. However, Grant, as of late, has been a controversial figure because of his public approach to reconciliation politics where he has to negotiate the boundaries of mainstream public acceptance, Indigenous advocacy and acceptance within the Indigenous community as a representative of Aboriginal experiences.

Indigenous Australians are expected to 'behave' in certain ways and assume specific roles when invited into the Australian national narrative. Elder et al. (2006), discussing the Sydney 2000 Olympics, explains how Indigenous voices who spoke out against the carefully constructed government and media narrative of a united, egalitarian nation were framed as 'deviant' and 'threatening'. Elder et al. argue that these voices were disciplined as a result. "Indigenous people had two choices: be docile and compliant … or speak out … and be vilified and demonized" (2006, p. 190). Similarly, Gardiner (2003) suggests that Indigenous athletes at the height of their careers are "expected to remain silent about racism and racial abuse" (p. 227). Indigenous athletes invited to participate in sport are "expected to relate to the consensus story of the level playing field" and "[t]heir invitation to be part of the nation is always conditional" (Elder, et.al., 2006, p. 186). That is, there is an onus on those who are marginalized to fit in to existing tropes and identity structures without challenge.

In Grant's case, in his early career he sought to establish himself as a 'professional' distancing himself from Indigenous issues and focusing on 'mainstream' stories because he did not want to be categorized as an 'Indigenous only' journalist for fear of being marginalized in his profession by losing 'mainstream' audiences. Grant's choice is reflected in *Talking to my Country* where he states, "I made a conscious decision that I would not be the 'indigenous reporter' … I wanted to be seen as a professional in my own right …" (2016, p. 126). He further highlights the need to establish an identity as "a credible reporter" in order to "have any impact [as a journalist] or be able to tell the stories of my own people" (Grant, 2016, p. 126). The problems were twofold when he did attempt to engage with Indigenous stories. Firstly, he had ethical issues trying to represent the lived experiences of those whose lives through his privileged position he did not share. Secondly, being an 'Indigenous reporter' covering 'Indigenous stories' did not garner the attention of 'mainstream' audiences (Grant, 2002). Thus, he needed the professional identity of the journalist.

The emphasis on establishing a 'professional', 'credible' identity in the media by Grant could indicate the effects of representations of the nation state on those whose identities sit on the periphery of constructed versions of the imaginary and the difficulties with challenging this narrative. In this instance, it is possible that Grant controls his image through the selection of stories to reinforce his identity as a professional and a journalist.

In the early 2000s, Grant left Australia following tabloid interest in his personal life because of an extramarital affair and took up an anchor role at CNN Hong Kong. Grant's time overseas significantly shifts his relationship with Australia and his personal identity. During his time overseas (2001-2012) Grant experienced acute depression, connecting the experiences of war and poverty that he witnessed as an international correspondent with the experiences of his people in Australia. In addition, he was no longer caught up in the politics that defined his identity when identifying as an Indigenous Australian or Wiradjuri man in Australia. Instead the burden of history and an Indigenous identity existing in an Australian national context was lifted, and he could claim an Australian identity in an uncomplicated way. Furthermore,

Grant's posting overseas continued to contribute to his establishment as a professional journalist in a 'mainstream' commercial media context.

After his time away, he publicly aligned more closely with his Indigenous identity explicitly through his media roles, speeches, writing and public appearances. He became host of *The Point* on National Indigenous Television (NITV). The nightly show covers topics significant to the lives of Aboriginal and Torres Strait Islander peoples, promoted as applying a different perspective to Australian news (NITV, 2016). In 2017, he was appointed as the ABC Editor of Indigenous Affairs. He also gained prominence through two public lectures. The first at the IQ2 debate by the Ethics Centre in October 2015, which attracted significant attention following its release online in January 2016 (The Ethics Centre, 2016). In this speech, Grant argues that the Australian dream is engrained in racism. The second speech was in July 2016, given at the University of New South Wales when Grant received an Honorary Doctorate of Letters (The University of NSW, 2016). In both speeches Grant drew on his personal narrative as an Indigenous person growing up in Australia, relating to audiences on a deeply human level. In these choices Grant is carefully pushing against the normalized Australian identity, as well as the normalized Indigenous Australian identity (those mentioned by Elder et al., 2006). He does this by appealing to the universality of human experience through the integration of his personal narrative with his political arguments. As a public figure who has been accepted within the 'normal' through his association with mainstream commercial media, Grant occupies a space within the normal discourse. By representing the experience of Indigeneity through his own - normalized – lens, he is slowly rephrasing the image of 'normality'. He also suggests that the 'normal' national narrative can shift if non-Indigenous peoples think about Indigenous issues through the more universal lens of humanity that he suggests through his references to 'my son', 'my family' in his writing and speeches.

However, in his contemporary advocate role, Grant negotiates a fine line. If he is too outspoken, his carefully constructed position both inside and outside the sphere of normality could be lost. This sentiment is echoed by Darumbul woman and journalist Amy McQuire (2016) who writes, "Aboriginal activists, thinkers and writers walk a fine line. Advocate too strongly and you face exclusion, compromise too often and you'll still end up with nothing" (2016). Critics have spoken out against Grant's discussion of colonial relations and his endeavors to have a national conversation on the legacies of colonialism and government policy (Bolt, 2016; Windschuttle, 2017). Alternatively, Grant's 'diplomatic', 'non-threatening' approach to engaging with race relations between Indigenous and non-Indigenous peoples has also been critiqued as placating white Australia, rather than challenging white privilege (McQuire,

2016). McQuire argues that Grant's approach is docile and compliant overshadowing those voices who are angry and outspoken. Grant thus operates in a difficult arena for advocating for Indigenous rights and recognition and pushing the 'normal' national narrative.

Adam Hills

Adam Hills is a comedian and media personality established in the United Kingdom (UK) as well as Australia. Between 2005 and 2011, he was host of the popular Australian music comedy quiz show *Spicks and Specks* on the ABC. The show earned Hills a nomination for a Gold Logie. Like Grant, Hills has also spent time abroad, establishing his career in the UK. First through stand-up comedy and frequent appearances at the Edinburgh Comedy Festival. Then, as a contributor to the *Ouch* blog on the British Broadcasting Corporation (BBC) web platform - a site geared towards discussing "disability" from a "fresh angle" (BBC, Ouch: Disability Talk).

In 2008, Hills was co-host of the Beijing Paralympics Games Opening and Closing Ceremony coverage on the ABC. He is currently the host of the television show *The Last Leg* on Channel 4 (and broadcast in Australia on ABC2), which has been revered for successfully pairing disability and comedy (Ryan, 2012). In his early career Hills emphasized his relatability to the audience; specifically, by identifying as an Australian, whose work celebrated larrikinism (embracing an attitude that mocks established authority) and in the delivery of "sun-drenched humour" (Saner, 2012). Hills' early decision to engage positive humor was his chosen marker of difference, resisting what he saw as the dominant trend in comedy to criticize through humor. Hills instead chose to celebrate his audience and fellow comedians (Saner, 2012). One of Hills' early successes beyond the stand-up comedy stage, came in 2002 when he released the charity single *Working Class Anthem*. This comedy single saw Hills retain the lyrics of the Australian national anthem but replace the music with the tune of *Working Class Man* by Jimmy Barnes. To Hills, this song's adaption was a better fit for the national anthem.

In this instance, Hills represents Australian audiences as predominantly associating with the words of the existing Australian anthem, but with the altered tune. It should be noted that the lyrics to the anthem have been criticized for the erasure of Aboriginal and Torres Strait Islander histories (Cheetham, 2015). Thus, the anthem constructs Australian identity as one of hegemonic whiteness and masculinity, an image that has been cultivated and maintained in wider media representations of typical 'Australian' manliness (Beasley, 2008).

Hills himself is a reflection of the hegemonic white masculine national identity in a number of significant ways, he is white, heterosexual, grew up in a suburban home and embraces sport (Saner, 2014). By these identifiers Hills reflects a number of the characteristics valued in the dominant narrative that informs the exclusionary representations of the 'typical Australian' in Australian media. Yet, Hill's position as a comedian with a prosthetic foot may destabilize dominant representations of the 'typical Australian'. For instance, in a piece describing his inability to wear thongs (toe sandals), Hills described himself as "retarded" (Hills, 2004a), but in a manner, which some observers characterize as questioning the power asymmetries created when reducing the national identity to a type of footwear (Giuffre, 2014). This suggests that despite embracing Australian markers of identity he is also outside of the 'look' associated with the Australian identity.

Conversely Hills' image also reinforces the dominant Australian identity. As one piece describes, "[t]all and tanned, Hills, who is married to an opera singer and has a young daughter, … [is] a man for whom the word "hunky" was surely invented" (Gordon, 2013), this representation of Hills reproduces the 'ideal Australian' as one of privilege. Hills' role in constructing this privileged identity is evidenced in his decision to represent himself as a comedian first before acknowledging or including humor about his prosthetic foot (Ellis 2016), a choice not available to many individuals whose markers of 'difference' are more overt.[2] However, Hills' decision to exclude disability needs to be positioned within an Australian media context and the effects of identifying with a disability. In their discussion of a newspaper article covering the parade organized following the 2000 Sydney Paralympics, Goggin and Newell highlight how the journalist focuses on establishing the different impairments of the athletes and how the impairment was acquired, arguing that this is part of "living with a disability in Australian society" (2005, p. 90). This is because "disability [is represented to] define ... [them], and ... private information about someone's disability is expected to be presented, and represented in public" (2005, p. 90). As part of this "we need to know what 'happened' to them - or 'what their disability is'…[t]o place a person with disability, to cope with their difference from someone who is 'normal'" (p. 90).

Hills embraced his marker of 'difference' in his comedy material only after he became established as a comedian. His prosthetic became a subject of his humor particularly after the increased airport security procedures were put in place subsequent to the 9/11 terrorist attacks in New York (Saner, 2012). In

---

[2] Early in his career, Hills had attempted to include the fact that he was born with one foot into his act, but was deterred by other comedians, his manager and also had his own reservations about being classified as a 'disabled comedian' (Ellis, 2016).

this instance, Hills' lived experience, whereby his prosthetic foot became unavoidably central to interactions with security personnel, became an opportunity to invite his audience into the experience of living with a 'non-normative' body. It perhaps also became a means through which Hills could invite his audiences into questioning or problematizing the securitization of bodies and national borders in response to the threat posed by terrorism following 9/11. Since this time, Hills has embraced themes and experiences of 'disability' and non-normative corporeality into his comedic material and career.

Subsequent to moving to the UK, Hills (in 2003) took a role on the *Ouch* blog for the BBC website discussing the attitudes, barriers and discrimination that people with disability face (2003; 2004a; 2004b; 2005a; 2005b). More recently Hills has become known in the UK through his hosting role on the show *The Last Leg*. Interestingly, Hills' media success in Australia does not reflect his engagement with impairment and disability politics to the same extent that these discussions were facilitated in the UK. This raises questions about acceptance of 'disability' in the Australian media when compared to the UK in regards to Hills' self-representation and engagement with disability.

Whilst Hills does not personally identify as someone with a 'disability' resisting the label he sees as focusing on the "inabilities" of people with "non-normative" bodies (Saner, 2012), he has accepted these roles where disability discussion and authority is required (Sperling, 2012). Given that Hills has now entered the UK media not only as a 'larrikin' comedian, but as a commentator on 'disability' and impairment through his UK hosting and blog positions questions must be asked. Hills fits with the Australian larrikin identity of the white, heterosexual, suburban, male and does not identify as someone with a 'disability'. The foregrounding and reception of Hills' perspective on disability in the UK suggests a broadening of the 'typical' Australian identity overseas. Yet, at the same time he still reflects the aforementioned identifiers of normalized Australian identity (white, heterosexual, suburban and male), and is recognized as an Australian larrikin comedian in the UK. It is thus possible that Hills both destabilizes and simultaneously reproduces the existing white male narrative that has traditionally been central to Australian media landscapes.

Dami Im

Dami Im is an Australian singer who won the reality singing competition *The X-Factor* in 2013. In 2016, she became Australia's most successful Eurovision entrant, placing second in the competition. Im was born in South Korea and migrated to Australia at the age of nine, settling in the Queensland town of

Logan. While her upbringing places her within an Australian context, her ethnic heritage is a highly visible means of marking her as an Other in an Australia dominated by Anglo-European visual imaginations.

Upon her *X-Factor* victory in 2013, Im attracted a number of racist comments via social media claiming her ethnicity prevented her from being an Australian pop singer (ABC news, 2013). Im sought to calm tensions between these members of the public and her fans by viewing the controversy as an educational opportunity (Byrnes, 2013). However, the reaction against her ethnicity illustrated that, as recently as 2013, the nation's image of what constitutes an 'Australian' identity is still highly contentious.

Media coverage of Im constructs her as predominantly 'Australian',[3] with an emphasis on her place of residence (Hunt, 2016) and her local school (Adams, 2016). This is particularly the case during the 2016 Eurovision competition as Im's background is described for uninitiated audiences. During the competition, both her status as 'Australian' and part of a 'multicultural' community are highlighted. In particular, she is 'claimed' as Australian through the linguistic marker 'our' (Zeiher, 2016). Her domestic status is also discussed using familiar Australian slang – 'hubby' to describe her husband – to increase her relatability to a general Australian audience. At the same time, her interest in high fashion is evoked to construct her as a fashionista. Im's public image is thus one of a migrant who has achieved the necessary level of integration into the Australian social fabric to be afforded the title of 'Australian'. While she is a "pop diva" (Byrnes, 2013a) and a fashionista, she is also a wife and Christian (Dwyer, 2016).

As a celebrity figure with a highly visible public persona, Dami Im's 'professional' identity is naturally emphasized. Indeed, her musical performances are locations of primary identification, the space where the celebrity is first encountered (O'Shaughnessy & Stadler, 2012). Thus, media representation of Im will naturally highlight her profession, and evaluate her quality as a singer. However, the construction of specific narratives of her private life, can be viewed as a means to make her Otherness 'safe' and acceptable. In essence, the construction of Im's private persona achieves a form of normalizing that shapes Im within hegemonic discourses.

Alongside Im's placement within the successful migrant narrative, is the creation of a private persona that conforms to hegemonic norms. Descriptions

---

[3] This section draws upon data collected for a piece in *Celebrity Studies Journal.* For more on methodology and results see Lam, C. (2018). Representing (real) Australia: Australia's Eurovision entrants, diversity and Australian identity. *Celebrity Studies*, DOI: 10.1080/19392397.2018.1432354

of Im as a wife, whose loving "hubby" (SBS, 2016) supports her musical endeavors reinforces her heteronormative status. Additionally, media reports that emphasize her love of fashion and creative approach to outfits, align her within a conventional model of femininity that highlights a "precious, ornamental and fragile" construction of women (Goffman, 1977, p. 311). Her identification as Christian also places her within a religiously dominant group. In the current context of elevated religious tensions, her affiliation with an 'acceptable' religion increases her degree of integration and inclusion. While she may be ethnically different, all other aspects of Im's persona are constructed (or emphasized) according to hegemonic norms, rendering her Otherness as relatively benign. The construction of Im's private persona thus strives to 'normalize' her as much as her ethnic divergence from the mainstream allows. In all other aspects, Im's life is presented as 'typical' in an effort to mitigate her Otherness and normalize her image.

While the media do play a role in the construction of Im's public (and private) image, Im herself is also a part of the construction of her normalized identity. Shortly after her victory on *The X-Factor* in 2013, the Seven Network produced a television special in which Im, and her mentor Dani Minogue, undertook a journey to (re)discover her cultural roots. The special not only introduced Im to a national audience, it cast her within a 'good migrant' narrative, wherein migration results in harmonious social integration (she is a proud Queenslander), success for the individual (her assent to pop stardom) and the ability to contribute to the new home country. While Im may not have demonstrated an ability to contribute in 2013, three years later she became "our Eurovision hope" (Molloy, 2016) as Australia's entrant. In placing second in the competition, she not only secured Australia's highest ranking to date, she also reinforced her ability to fulfil the model of a successful migrant by contributing to the success of the nation. Indeed, during the competition, she is characterized as an exemplar of multiculturalism and "the power of immigration" by Australia's Ambassador to Sweden (2016 Eurovision host) during a showcase at the Australian Embassy. Reporting on the event, SBS journalist Chris Zeiher notes that amidst the European refugee crisis the "point [was] not lost on [the] European crowd" (2016). Im is thus able to fulfil the narrative of a successful immigration policy by performing her difference from the mainstream within what Laura Moran terms the "celebratory language of tolerance" (2016, p. 714). Yet, this difference is 'tolerated' insofar as it does not disrupt the (white) mainstream national identity. Concurrently, Im's religious affiliations (Christian), domestic situation (married) and display of femininity (as a fashionista), all reinforce hegemonic norms that construct her as a 'safe' alternative within the mainstream, which does not threaten the imagined national identity.

Conclusion

Once absorbed into the 'norm', Grant is now positioned outside as a Wiradjuri man who is also an established and middle class Australian media professional. Despite engaging his 'difference' Grant is simultaneously performing in a manner that maintains his 'safe' identity within the 'norm'. As a result, he now seeks to deepen the identities within the 'norm' but in a manner that navigates and negotiates the structure of 'norm' and what it excludes. Grant uses his personal narrative as a means to include a historically excluded and contemporarily marginalized (Indigenous) identity into the 'norm'.

Grant acknowledges his privilege, which is positioned as the 'norm'. However, he also positions privilege as not separate to Aboriginality. This is the shift in representation that Grant's identity as a celebrity manifests and posits as an alternative 'normal' national identity. For Grant, his privilege is something, which resonates even when he engages his 'non-normal' feelings about Indigenous rights. As a result, he is seeking to deepen the center, inviting people in to relate as human beings, but in this act also reifies the identity positioned in the center. Grant sits on the fringes of the national 'norm' trying not to 'other' himself but remains aware of how Aboriginal and Torres Strait Islander peoples are marginalized in Australia, thereby creating a risk that he could isolate himself from the 'norm' and undermine his ability to deepen the narrative.

Hills sits in many ways within the 'norm' and comfortably started within this sphere. Unless Hills chooses to reveal his difference, he is the face of the mainstream in many ways. Hills' position of challenging the 'normal' is quite safe because he does through trying to invite people in on the joke, and through obscuring his 'disability'. He can thus, inhabit both 'normal' and 'non-normal' spheres at will, unlike many others with disability or those who are unable to obscure their 'difference'.

Im is visually marked as different, thus to enter the sphere of 'normality', she performs what is constructed as being 'normal' in mainstream Australian media. With the exception of her (visually different) ethnicity, she aligns with other markers of 'normality': her accent, heterosexuality, fashionista status as model of femininity, Christianity. Additionally, her publicized lived experience aligns with a national narrative that is constructed for those of difference; in her case the 'good migrant' narrative.

These case studies demonstrate a different trajectory for all three Australian celebrities that have been shaped by their relationship to the normalized Australian national identity, which is further explored in Jackie Raphael and Celia Lam's chapter on Chris Hemsworth in this volume. This framework makes clear that Grant, as an Indigenous broadcaster and journalist who has increasingly shifted into the role of advocate for Indigenous rights, is both inside and outside the 'normal' national identity in an attempt to provide an alternative space for recognizing Australia's problematic past with Indigenous Australians. Hills is located predominantly in the center as a white, heterosexual, middle-class male who does not consider himself a person with a 'disability'. Hills seeks to subtly expand the boundaries to include the types of bodies, which have been excluded from media representations of the 'normal' identity. Im's identifiers of difference were made explicit prior to celebrity status. She thus sits outside the representation of 'normal' and has to anchor herself to established values in order to 'enter' normalized representations of the Australian national identity. What this chapter makes clear is that contemporary 'Australian identity' is still governed by the social and immigration policies established in the early 20th century that privilege whiteness, maleness and 'able-bodies'. This notion of Australian identity is perpetuated through media discourses, whilst simultaneously governing how Australian celebrities self-represent, and are subsequently represented in the Australian media.

References

ABC News. (2013). Asian-Australian X Factor winner Dami Im thankful for support after racist taunts. *ABC news*. Retrieved January 5, 2018, from http://www.abc.net.au/news/2013-10-29/an-x-factor-australia-winner-dami-im/5054090

Adams, C. (2016). Your dummies guide to the long history and strict rules of Eurovision before Dami Im sings for Australia. *News.com.au*. Retrieved January 5, 2018, from http://www.news.com.au/entertainment/music/your-dummies-guide-to-the-long-history-and-strict-rules-of-eurovision-before-dami-im-sings-for-australia/news-story/c5fcfd38cbe9978882dcd9737cc3e1db

Akbarzadeh, S. (2016). The Muslim question in Australia: Islamophobia and Muslim alienation. *Journal of Muslim Minority Affairs, 36*(3), 323-333.

Atherfold, J. (2006). Redfern: the "riot" and the reporting. *Australian Studies in Journalism, 17*, 41-53.

Australian Government Department of Environment and Energy. (n.d.). *National heritage places - Myall Creek massacre and memorial site*. Retrieved January 24, 2018, from http://www.environment.gov.au/heritage/places/national/myall-creek.

Beasley, C. (2008). Rethinking hegemonic masculinity in a globalizing world. *Men and Masculinities, 11*(1), 86-103.

Bird, D. (1983). Australian woman: A national joke? *Australian Journal of Cultural Studies, 1*(1), 111-114.

Bolt, A. (2016). Stan Grant's view on Australia is too black and white. *The Herald Sun.* Retrieved January 5, 2018, from http://www.heraldsun.com.au/news/opinion/andrew-bolt/stan-grants-view-on-australia-is-too-black-and-white/news-story/1486baaef570c178fdfd710473780b95.

British Broadcasting Corporation. (n.d.). Ouch: Disability talk. *BBC.* Retrieved December 5, 2017, from http://www.bbc.co.uk/programmes/p05p07rq.

Byrnes, H. (2013). X Factor victor Dami Im wants to bridge cultural gap and calms racism row. *News.com.au.* Retrieved January 5, 2018, from http://www.news.com.au/entertainment/tv/x-factor-victor-dami-im-wants-to-bridge-cultural-gap-and-calms-racism-row/news-story/fe1b80cd2474e2a6e5bdf40d2db2134d.

Byrnes, H. (2013a). X Factor Australia top 10 moments. *News.com.au.* Retrieved January 5, 2018, from http://www.news.com.au/entertainment/tv/x-factor-australia-top-10-moments/story-e6frfmyi-1226748336895.

Cheetham, D. (2015). Young and free? Why I declined to sing the national anthem at the 2015 AFL grand final. *The Conversation.* Retrieved January 5, 2018, from http://theconversation.com/young-and-free-why-i-declined-to-sing-the-national-anthem-at-the-2015-afl-grand-final-49234.

Curthoys, A. (2009). White, British, and European: historicising identity in settler societies. In J. Carey, and C., McLisky (Eds.), *Creating white Australia* (pp. 3-24). NSW, Sydney: Sydney University Press.

Dwyer, G. (2016). Why Dami Im is the perfect choice to be Australia's 2016 Eurovision star. *SBS.com.au.* Retrieved January 5, 2018, from https://www.sbs.com.au/programs/eurovision/article/2016/03/02/why-dami-im-perfect-choice-be-australias-2016-eurovision-star.

Elder, C., Pratt, A. & Ellis, C. (2006). Running race: Reconciliation, nationalism and the Sydney 2000 Olympic Games. *International Review for the Sociology of Sport, 41*(2), 181-200.

Ellis, K. (2016). *Disability media work: Opportunities and obstacles.* New York: Palgrave Macmillan US.

Gardiner, G. (2003). Running for country: Australian print media representation of Indigenous athletes in the 27th Olympiad. *Journal of Sport & Sport Issues, 27*(3), 233-260.

Gargett, A. (2005). A critical media analysis of the Redfern riot. *Indigenous Law Bulletin, 6*(10), 8-11.

Giuffre, L. (2015). #IsItOk to be a celebrity (disabled) comedian?: Approaching disability with Adam Hills's television programme, *The Last Leg.* In D. Jackson,

C. E. M. Hodges, M. Molesworth & R. Scullion (Eds.), *Reframing disability? Media, (Dis)Empowerment and Voice in the 2012 Paralympics* (pp. 66-78). New York, Oxon: Routledge.

Goffman, E. (1977). The Arrangement between the sexes. *Theory and Society, 4,* 301-331.

Goggin, G. & Newell, C. (2005). *Disability in Australia: Exposing a social apartheid.* NSW, Sydney: UNSW Press.

Gordon, B. (2013). What do you call a comic with a positive slant? Adam Hills. *The Telegraph.* Retrieved February 13, 2017 from http://www.telegraph.co.uk/culture/comedy/9865197/What-do-you-call-a-comic-with-a-positive-slant-Adam-Hills.html

Grant, S. (2004). *The tears of strangers: A family memoir.* Australia: HarpersCollins*Publishers.*

Grant, S. (2016). *Talking to my country.* Australia: HarpersCollins*Publishers.*

Hall, S. (1980). Encoding and decoding. In. S. Hall, D. Hobson, A. Lowe & P. Willis (Eds.). *Culture, media, language* (pp. 128-138). London: Hutchinson.

Henderson, L. (2017). Popular television and public mental health: creating media entertainment from mental distress. *Critical Public Health, 28*(1)*,* 106-117.

Hills, A. (2003). Sign here if you're normal [online]. *Ouch! BBC.* Retrieved January 15, 2018, from http://www.bbc.co.uk/ouch/features/sign_here_if_youre_normal.shtml

Hills, A. (2004 a). One foot on the beach [online]. *Ouch! BBC.* Retrieved January 24, 2017, from: http://www.bbc.co.uk/ouch/features/one_foot_on_the_beach.shtml.

Hills, A. (2004 b). The Hillsy Corporation: exposed! [online]. *Ouch! BBC.* Retrieved January 11, 2018, from http://www.bbc.co.uk/ouch/features/sign_here_if_youre_normal.shtml

Hills, A. (2004 c). Prosthesis Envy [online]. *Ouch! BBC.* Retrieved January 17, 2018, from: http://www.bbc.co.uk/ouch/features/prosthesis_envy.shtml.

Hills, A. (2005 a). When is a joke not a joke? [online]. *Ouch! BBC.* Retrieved January 13, 2018, from http://www.bbc.co.uk/ouch/opinion/when_is_a_joke_not_a_joke.shtml

Hills, A. (2005 b). Head over heel [online]. *Ouch! BBC.* Retrieved January 17, 2018, from http://www.bbc.co.uk/ouch/features/head_over_heel.shtml

Hogan, J. (2010). Gendered and racialised discourses of national identity in Baz Luhrmann's Australia. *Journal of Australian Studies, 34*(1), 63-77.

Hollinsworth, D. (2005). "My Island Home": Riot and resistance in media representations of Aboriginality. *Social Alternatives, 24*(1), 16-20.

Hunt, E. (2016). Australia's Dami Im would have won Eurovision under last year's voting system. *The Guardian.* Retrieved January 5, 2018, from https://www.theguardian.com/tv-and-radio/2016/may/18/australias-dami-im-would-have-won-eurovision-under-last-years-voting-system

Korff, J. (2017). Myall Creek massacre (1838). *Creative Spirits.* Retrieved January 24, 2018, from https://www.creativespirits.info/aboriginalculture/history/myall-creek-massacre-1838

Johanson, K. & Glow, H. (2009). Honour bound in Australia: From defensive nationalism to critical nationalism. *National Identities, 11*(4), 385-396.

Lake, M. (1997). Women and nation in Australia: The politics of representation. *Australian Journal of Politics & History, 43*(1), 41-52.

Langton, M. (2008). Trapped in the Aboriginal reality show. *Griffith REVIEW, 19*, 143-162.

McCann, J. & Wilson, J. (2014). Representation of women in Australian parliaments. Research paper series 2014-2015. 9 July 2014. *Department of Parliamentary Services.* Retrieved December 12, 2017, from http://parlinfo.aph.gov.au/parlInfo/download/library/prspub/3269009/upload_binary/3269009.pdf;fileType=application/pdf

McQuire, A. (2016). The viral rise Of Stan Grant: Why diplomacy won't be enough for our people. *newmatilda.com.* Retrieved October 8, 2017, from https://newmatilda.com/2016/02/26/the-dizzying-rise-of-stan-grant-why-diplomacy-wont-be-enough-for-our-people/.

McRobbie, A. (2005). *The uses of cultural studies: A textbook.* London: Sage.

Meadows, M. (1995). Sensitivity not censorship: reporting cultural diversity in Australia. *Australian Journalism Review, 17*(2), 18-27.

Meadows, M. (2004). Media images of Indigenous affairs in Australia. In J. Leigh and E. Loo (Eds), *Outer Limits: A reader in communication across cultures* (pp 273-289). Victoria, Melbourne: Language Australia.

Meadows, M., & Morris, C. (1998). Into the new millennium: the role of Indigenous media in Australia. *Media International Australia, 88*, 67-78.

Molloy, S. (2016). Our Eurovision hope Dami Im goes full circle in Sweden, where she wrote her hit album two years ago. *News.com.au.* Retrieved January 5, 2018, from http://www.news.com.au/entertainment/tv/our-eurovision-hope-dami-im-goes-full-circle-in-sweden-where-she-wrote-her-hit-album-two-years-ago/news-story/bae04b6243e961f21766db153d3845bd.

Moran, L. (2016). Constructions of race: Symbolic ethnic capital and the performance of youth identity in multicultural Australia, *Ethnic and Racial Studies, 39* (4), 708-726.

Morley, D. (1992). *Television. Audiences and cultural Studies.* London: Routledge.

NITV. (2016). How to watch The Point with Stan Grant. *NITV.* Retrieved December 5, 2017, from, https://www.sbs.com.au/nitv/the-point-with-stan-grant/article/2016/02/25/how-watch-point-stan-grant.

O'Shaughnessy, M., & Stadler, J. (2012). *Media and Society* (5th ed.). Victoria, Melbourne: Oxford University Press.

Rowe, R., Tilbury, F., Rapley, M. & O' Ferrall, I. (2003). 'About a year before the breakdown I was having symptoms'; Sadness, pathology and the Australian newspaper media. *Sociology of Health & Illness, 55*(6), 680-696.

Ryan, F. (2012). The Last Leg: often tasteless, sometimes awkward, always funny. *The Guardian.* Retrieved February 18, 2918, from https://www.theguardian.com/tv-and-radio/tvandradioblog/2012/sep/05/the-last-leg-tasteless-awkward-funny.

Saner, E. (2012). Australian comedian Adam Hills: 'I was born without a foot. Dull. Move on'. *The Guardian.* Retrieved August 25, 2017, from https://www.theguardian.com/theguardian/2012/aug/24/adam-hills-comedian-disability-tv-paralympics.

SBS. (2016). Dami Im's hubby Noah is her loving support at Eurovision 2016. *SBS.* Retrieved January 5, 2018, from http://www.sbs.com.au/ondemand/video/684325443967/dami-ims-hubby-noah-is-her-loving-support-at-eurovision-2016.

Screen Australia. (2016). *Seeing ourselves: Reflections on diversity in Australian TV drama.* Retrieved January 5, 2018, from https://www.screenaustralia.gov.au/getmedia/157b05b4-255a-47b4-bd8b-9f715555fb44/TV-Drama-Diversity.pdf.

Smith, P. & Phillips, T. (2006). Collective belonging and mass media consumption: unravelling how technological medium and cultural genre shapes the national imaginings of Australians. *The Sociological Review, 54*(4), 818-846.

Soldatic, K. & Fiske, L. (2009). Bodies 'locked up': intersections of disability and race in Australian immigration detention. *Disability & Society, 24*(3), 289-301.

Sperling, D. (2012) Frankie Boyle Paralympics jokes defended by Games presenter Adam Hills. Adam Hills says Boyle's jokes were acceptable: "Paralympians can be offensive too". *Digital Spy.* 5 September. Retrieved January 5, 2018, from http://www.digitalspy.com/showbiz/comedy/news/a403937/frankie-boyle-paralympics-jokes-defended-by-games-presenter-adam-hills/.

The Ethics Centre. (2016). *Stan Grant's speech on racism and the Australian dream.* Retrieved January 27, 2017, from http://www.ethics.org.au/on-ethics/blog/january-2016/stan-grant-s-speech-on-racism-and-the-australian-d.

The University of NSW. (2016). *Stan Grant Wallace Wurth lecture: From reconciliation to rights.* Retrieved January 27, 2017, from https://www.youtube.com/watch?v=qnNe-YzGaEI.

Thomas, M. (2017). The 1967 Referendum. *Parliamentary Library FlagPost.* Retrieved February 21, 2018 from https://www.aph.gov.au/About_Parliament/Parliamentary_Departments/Parliamentary_Library/FlagPost/2017/May/The_1967_Referendum

Watson Jnr, S. (1978). Blacks and the media. *Social Alternatives, 1*(3), 27-28.

Windshuttle, K. (2017). Let Cook and Macquarie stand: Grant and Taylor are wrong. *The Australian.* Retrieved November 8, 2017, from http://www.theaustralian.com.au/news/inquirer/let-cook-and-macquarie-stand-grant-and-taylor-are-wrong/news-story/40b157aac543734a6e0417b1397c3ec7.

Zeiher, C. (2016). Dami Dazzles the crowd in Stockholm at Australian embassy party. *SBS.* Retrieved January 5, 2018, from http://www.sbs.com.au/programs/eurovision/article/2016/05/10/dami-dazzles-crowd-stockholm-australian-embassy-party

Harnessing celebrity to fight casual racism: A thematic analysis of responses to Taika Waititi's "Give nothing to racism" campaign

Angelique Nairn and Frances Nelson

Abstract. In 2017, *Hunt for the Wilderpeople* director, Taika Waititi was named New Zealander of the year (stuff.co.nz, 2017). Since then he has lent his celebrity brand to the creation and dissemination of the Human Rights Campaign "Give nothing to racism" (Black, 2017; Warhurst, 2017). It is not uncommon for celebrities to engage in advocacy: their public personas can "crystallise issues" (Marshall, 2013, p. 370) and move audiences to action (Marshall, 2013; O'Regan, 2014). In essence, celebrities function as a site of identification (Noland, Goodale, Marshall, & Schlecht, 2009), because people form attachments to the mediated images of those they admire and with whom they perceive a commonality (Burke, 1969). Such identification can encourage individuals to emulate the behaviors of celebrities (Petty & Cacioppo, 1984). Therefore, by being authentic and credible in their advocacy, celebrities can persuade ordinary people to do the extra-ordinary and help in solving society's problems (Goodman & Barnes, 2011). However, there is much conjecture over celebrities' 'true' influence in social issues and whether they can positively impact audiences (O'Regan, 2014). Furthermore, their support of issues can be considered token and superficial (Noland, et al., 2009). The purpose of this research, then, is to use thematic analysis (Braun & Clarke, 2006) to examine the online, and particularly social media responses, of New Zealanders, firstly in relation to the campaign "Give nothing to racism" and secondly, to Taika Waititi's involvement. The intention of the research was to determine the attitudes of audiences to the issue of race and whether they believe Waititi's inclusion and approach to the issue were appropriate.

Keywords: public service announcement, Taika Waititi, celebrity advocacy, racism, social media

Introduction

It is a common practice among organizations responsible for public service announcements to enhance the credibility of the message by selecting a well-known person to be its 'face' (Panis & Van den Bulck, 2012, 2014). It is a simple strategy based on borrowing the resources, popularity and respect of the public figure (Marshall, 2013; Meyer & Gamson, 1995; Panis & Van den Bulck, 2012), although it has some perils: fame can turn to notoriety (Garcia de los Salmones, Dominguez & Herrero, 2013; Noland, et al., 2009; Partzsch, 2015; Wheeler, 2014), and of course, public reactions to the chosen celebrity are a matter of individual perception (Panis & Van den Bulck, 2012). In early 2017, Taika Waititi was named "New Zealand of the Year" (McKee, 2017), and in the middle of the year, he fronted a public service campaign called "Give nothing to racism" for the Human Rights Commission (Black, 2017; Warhurst, 2017). Waititi and the Human Rights Commission hoped that the video would draw attention to what it called "casual racism" (Black, 2017) and invested in the campaign because about one third of the complaints it received were about racism. The Commission said, "Many Kiwis don't think racism is a problem. Yet those of us who don't consider ourselves 'racist' still allow casually racist thoughts / actions / comments in our lives" (Black, 2017). On the face of it, Taika Waititi is a perfect match for the anti-racism message. He is famous both in Aotearoa-New Zealand and abroad, and his creative credentials are extensive[1], but as well as his achievements in entertainment, in 2015 he worked for the charity Cure Kids and other organizations fighting child poverty (Howie, 2017; Maori Television, n.d.). He was also the director of an earlier public service announcement called *Blazed*, which uses humor to raise awareness of the dangers of drug driving, and in fact, a certain "sly humor" (Black, 2017) is a marker of his style.

The Race Relations Commissioner, Dame Susan Devoy, pronounced herself "chuffed" (Newshub.co.nz, 2017) by Waititi's video, saying approvingly:

> It's not about hate, it's about hope. He said racism starts small - but it doesn't have to start at all… I thought we were a much more tolerant country than we are, and I think as Kiwis we pride ourselves on giving everyone a fair go - but this is an opportunity to put that into action.

Official approval of the video, then, was swift and unanimous, but public reactions were, perhaps predictably, mixed. It is the purpose of this paper to use Taika Waititi's video as a case study to examine public reaction to the deployment of a celebrity "brand" (Panis & Van den Bulck, 2012). To this end, we analyzed three thousand posts on Facebook to establish whether themes (Braun & Clarke, 2006) could be found in the public's identification and disidentification (Basil, 1996; Cashmore, 2006) with the message.[2]

---

[1] Taika Waititi is well known in Aotearoa-New Zealand as a story-teller, writer and actor (Maori Television, n.d; NZONSCREEN, n.d.). His work richly expresses multiple facets of the country's culture and identity, including a particularly laconic "Kiwi" humour (Howie, 2017; stuff.co.nz, 2017). He is famous for *Boy (*2010), and his *Hunt for the Wilderpeople* (2016) was New Zealand's "most successful film ever" (Maori Television, n.d.).

[2] Data was retrieved from https://www.facebook.com/taika.waititi/videos/1398955706817658/ and https://www.facebook.com/NZHumanRightsCommission/videos/237124230118464/.

Literature review

According to Kerrigan et al. (2011), a personal brand is an exercise in managing others' perceptions so as to accomplish personal ambitions and goals. An established brand narrative becomes the public "embodiment of the artist" (Preece & Kerrigan, 2015, p. 1208) that paints a particular picture of the 'name' and associated reputation, image, signature style and credibility (Elsbach, 2009; Preece & Kerrigan, 2015). Obviously, the nature of any celebrity's personal brand is the deciding factor in asking that person to front a particular cause, but the power of celebrity brands can be so great that Goodman and Barnes (2011, p. 72) argue, "celebrities are now cast in the formative role of deciding who and what are worthy of being saved or developed." Celebrities-as-brands, then, have considerable communicative power (Kogen, 2015; Meyer & Gamson, 1995; Panis & Van den Bulck, 2014; Partzsch, 2015; Thrall, et al., 2008) and so can influence audiences on given issues (Cashmore, 2006; O'Regan, 2014; Partzsch, 2015) by transmitting strong feelings through direct and indirect means of persuasion (Garcia de los Salmones, Dominguez & Herrero, 2013; Marshall, 2013).

There does need to be a perceptible fit between celebrities' brands and the social issues (Panis & Van den Bulck, 2014), because, according to Toncar, Reid and Anderson (2007), the credibility of the celebrity is paramount if the message is to be completely effective. Credibility depends on demonstrating personal knowledge of the cause and expressing objective opinions (Toncar, et al., 2007). Garcia de los Salmones, Dominguez and Herrero (2013, p. 113) put it this way, "If people perceive some type of link between the celebrity and the social cause, the expertise and trustworthiness of the celebrity will not be questioned". A message has more chance of positive reception if the defining antecedent condition of success is met: that is, strong congruence between the celebrity and the issue and organization (Toncar et al. 2007). Although a good fit between the celebrity and the cause is essential, another factor that can influence the positive reception of the message is the general attractiveness of the spokesperson. Toncar et al. (2007), for instance, found that audiences consider attractive spokespeople to be similar and familiar to them, and consequently more likeable.

It is easy to see why organizations employ charismatic celebrities to be their public faces (Marshall, 2013; O'Regan, 2014; Noland, et al., 2009; Panis & Van den Bulck, 2012; Thrall, et al. 2008; Toncar, et al., 2007), but as well as any material reward (Panis & Van den Bulck, 2012), association with a worthy cause is beneficial to the celebrities also, in various intangible ways. For instance, Garcia de los Salmones, et al., (2013) suggest that being associated with a good cause gives celebrities greater control over their brands, the opportunity to differentiate themselves positively in the crowded celebrity arena, and the chance to promote their image in a desirable way. Goodman and Barnes (2011, p. 81) suggest that the exercise of "(re)branding as 'caring', 'helping', 'authentic' and authoritative'" develops a new brand for the celebrity, and O'Regan (2014) argues that building the credibility of a cause simultaneously builds celebrities' own credibility. In fact, such is the usefulness of social activism to the positive establishing or development of brand that Thrall et al. (2008) found that of the celebrities they canvased, 68.2% supported some form of social activism. Noland et al. (2009, p. 207) propose that the adoption of a cause is a "mandatory rite of passage" for celebrities, and Panis and Van den Bulck (2014, p. 24) suggest that being a spokesperson for a cause is now "part of every celebrity's job description". In a similar vein, Goodman and Barnes (2011) maintain that engagement in some form of activism is simply one more part of performing celebrity.

The enactment of social engagement need not be based on pure motives to achieve the desired positive effect on celebrities' brand, for as Panis and Van den Bulck, (2012, p. 76) say, "When a celebrity supports a social cause, he/she additionally creates a socio-political image or persona, either from personal conviction and a need for self-fulfilment, or from a utilitarian attempt at self-promotion". Thus, in public service announcements, the relationship between celebrity cause, and public may be seen as symbiotic. To some extent, all parties in the relationship feed on and benefit in their own ways: the celebrity in terms of material reward and brand enhancement, the cause from a strong and winning message, and the public from a clear message of normative behaviors. In particular, those members of the public receptive to the message of the public service announcement, can feel a sense of commonality with one another, unifying, in this case, against racism. In this instance, the celebrity represents the ideals of the government, and if their involvement and the announcement are supported by the public, it can produce a sense of identity, unity and social cohesion (Anderson, 1983).

On the face of it, using celebrities as spokespeople offers such benefits that it seems simple common sense to employ them, but Toncar et al. (2007) warn that it can be a hazardous strategy. For instance, the fame of the celebrities can obscure the message, which in the face of the Elaboration Likelihood Model (Petty & Cacioppo, 1984), is problematic because a message has persuasive influence only when it is critically assessed and understood. Furthermore, though celebrities' presence might encourage short-term public interest in an issue, their involvement does not necessarily keep the issue newsworthy (Meyer & Gamson, 1995; Panis & Van den Bulck, 2014; Thrall, et al. 2008), and Panis and Van den Bulck (2014) argue that in fact, fewer than half the celebrities employed as spokespeople earn the cause any media coverage at all.

Indeed, according to Toncar et al. (2007), celebrities can reduce memory of the message to nothing but their presence, so to be useful to the cause, the celebrity needs to exhibit an active, lasting connection or be seen as insincere, and merely exploiting an opportunity for public attention (Garcia de los Salmones, et al., 2013; Noland, et al., 2009; Panis & Van den Bulck, 2012; Partzsch, 2015). Some celebrities deliberately affiliate with uncontroversial and "bandwagon" social issues to reduce potential risk to their reputations from associating with a polarizing cause (Meyer & Gamson, 1995; Panis & Van den Bulck, 2014; Partzsch, 2015). Another caveat against using celebrities comes from Kogen (2015), who warns that celebrities may oversimplify the issues that they front. On a related point, Panis and Van den Bulck (2012) observe, "… engaging a celebrity supporter may lead non-profit organisations to simplify or de-radicalise their message". O'Regan (2014) and Panis and Van den Bulck, (2014) assert there is a correlation between the 'pulling power' of the celebrity and the importance the public will assign to the cause.

The medium arguably makes a difference to message reception and perceptions of its authenticity. For instance, scholars maintain that some forms of social media encourage users to develop intense parasocial relationships with celebrities (Horton & Wohl, 1956; Marshall, 2010; Rubin & McHugh, 1987). Social media increases connectivity to the stars and the resultant parasocial relationships have two effects: first, to enhance the celebrities' credibility (Wheeler, 2014); and second, to 'fix' audiences in the cause (Bennett, 2014). Social media afford celebrities the ability to by-pass news media and communicate directly with audiences (Bennett, 2014), creating what Beer (2008, p. 232) calls a "perception of proximity", which can be used "adventurously" (Bennett, 2014, p. 149) to bring about feelings of belonging, and through that, direct action for the cause. Although Thrall et al. (2008) warn that online messages can be lost in the massive, noisy, competitive sprawl of cyberspace, in a real sense, social media allow controversial issues to garner support (Wheeler, 2014).

Method & methodology

Braun and Clark (2006, p. 78) assert that thematic analysis is so useful and versatile for dealing with a large bulk of data that it constitutes a "foundational method in qualitative analysis" that can be applied across a number of theoretical orientations. Broadly speaking, thematic analysis involves working systematically within a data set to find patterns and connections (Attride-Stirling, 2001; Lacey & Luff, 2001), which can then be grouped into categories of likeness called themes (Boyatzis, 1998; Fereday & Muir-Cochrane, 2006; Leininger, 1985; Liamputtong & Ezzy, 2005). The process of finding themes within a large data set should not be one of starting with a pre-formed coding frame. Instead, according to Boyatzis (1998) and Fereday and Muir-Cochrane (1996), researchers should work directly and relexively in the raw data and let connections form. Furthermore, because "data are not coded in an epistemological vacuum" (Braun & Clarke, 2006, p. 84), researchers should also accept and account for the fact that they themselves will be present in the final themes. A meaningful theme should not only delineate the categories in the data, but should also allow interpretation of both manifest and latent aspects of the phenomenon (Attride-Stirling, 2001; Boyatzis, 1998; Vaismoradi Jones, Turunen & Snelgrove, 2016).

A key decision in inductive thematic analysis is whether the aim of the research is to provide "a rich description of the data set or a detailed account of one particular aspect" (Braun & Clarke, 2006, p. 83). The raw data in this research consisted of 2436 applicable[3] Facebook posts engendered by Taika Waititi's "Give nothing to racism" campaign. The posts were subjected to inductive thematic analysis (Boyatzis, 1998), which has the benefit of letting the data drive the analysis, and in this case, permitted the formation of an holistic overview of the 'Taika Effect'. Importantly, the inductive approach means that the analysis did not proceed along pre-determined theoretic lines.

Thematic analysis presents some difficulties, in part because of the lack of a single established and agreed method (Braun & Clarke, 2006; Liamputtong & Ezzy, 2005; Vaismoradi, et al., 2016). In order to develop a solid and reliable coding process, we worked separately at first. Our process was to read the posts, become familiar with them and assign tentative codes based on key words and subjects. Still working separately, we observed whether and how codes began to coalesce into bigger groups. We both recorded 'quotable' posts that seemed to capture emerging themes. Although the number of posts in a code was not the determinant of a theme, we found we had tallied similar numbers of posts around key words, and we then linked codes into initial themes with provisional names.

Data analysis: The themes

The following section sets out the five themes that emerged from the data, describing the qualities of feeling and the ideas that coalesced in the coding. As well as expanding on the key words, each theme contains illustrative verbatim quotes from the posts. The themes from Taika Waititi's page were

---

[3] There were a number of posts that were irrelevant to the discussion (i.e. spam), which were excluded from the final analysis.

predominately about the man: one of unqualified support, which we called *Great Guy, Great Message* and one of equally unqualified disapproval, named *How Could They Get This So Wrong?* These themes were also apparent on the Human Rights Commission page, but an additional three themes were identified: *I Just Don't Get It*, comprising posts by people who could not grasp the irony, and thought the how-to-do-racism advice was serious; *Hate, Oh How I Hate*, which is made up primarily of racist messages and vicious personal attacks; and finally, *Every Little Thing*, in which posters used the video as a springboard into wider philosophy and other conversations.

Great Guy, Great Message

This theme expressed support for the message and the man. It comprises 1180 positive posts across both Facebook pages. Many of the posters in this category felt helped by the message, often because it resonated with their own experiences. One poster, for instance, said, "This is awesome. I'm Indian and have felt pressure to chuckle at so many racist comments made within the lame disguise of a joke… Taika Waititi so on point, so very much appreciated." This person clearly felt that she might now be able to amend previously reluctant participation in the 'soft racism' that occurs in pointed humor, and wrote a post that was whole-heartedly approving.

In an equally approving post, another person wrote, "What a clever video. Hard to find the typical racism excuse after watching that. Big ups to a worthy conversation and one of the good guys". Here, the post combines approval of the message and of the man, and points out the value of the campaign as "a worthy conversation". Another post said, "This is bloody awesome. So clever and funny and so very spot on". This idea is echoed by other posters, who found the message clever in itself and relevant to other social issues:

Sometimes the approval was indirect and contained a distinctly nationalistic self-congratulatory note: "NZ coming through with another great campaign!", but as a general rule, support of Taika Waititi was direct and strong. Several posters noted that this video is another expression of his signature style: "In typical Taika style, this addresses the issue in a unique way that grabs your attention & makes you listen - love this guy!" Sometimes the man and message elicit promises of particular behavior: "…I will do my part Taika! You're the man, bro!", but they mostly provoke straightforward appreciation of the style and the script of the message: "Done in a way that only Taika can do it! Creative, humorous but also thought provoking". Sometimes the posts are more exclamatory than thoughtful, but nevertheless contribute to the theme of approval: "OH MY LORD! His Legend Status BUUUUILDS ♥". Therefore, *Great Guy And Great Message* was not a difficult category to code, because when approval was given, it was unstinting and unmistakable. The posts in the next theme, *How Could They Get This So Wrong?* were also straightforward to identify, because they were as vehemently opposed to the man, the message or both.

How Could They Get This So Wrong?

This is the second theme and it was initially observed on Taika Waititi's own Facebook page where 18 posters objected to either the message or the involvement of Taika Waititi. On the Human Rights Commission Facebook page, the number of objectors was 114. It was obvious, then, that disapproval was a far smaller category than approval. Although the posts were not as numerous as those in the previous theme, however the language used suggests that the opinions were strongly felt.

A key thought that emerged was that it is not appropriate to use humor to highlight such a serious matter as racism: "This is why I am uncomfortable around kiwis... too many jokes about very real problems." On the same tack, another person posted, "I get the irony and sarcasm.... but no. Irony and sarcasm are not effective ways to help the world with kindness, love and respect." For these people, the humour was offensive, and because the video exemplified Taika Waititi's signature style, the disapproval extended beyond the message towards the choice of the man himself. Another aspect of disapproval of the message that occurred in this theme was the reverse of the nationalistic pride in the first theme: "What is wrong with u kiwis?". Here, the disapproval extends to the whole nation, which is blamed for a perceived error of judgment made by Taika Waititi in his composition and delivery of the message. It seemed that the writer was quite unaware that the stance adopted in this disapproving comment could itself easily be interpreted as racist.

On Taika Waititi as the 'face' for an anti-racism message, the posters followed two main lines of thought. The first idea that occurred is that Taika Waititi himself makes racist jokes, especially against Australians: "What about the Aussie jibes on Flight of the Concords?" and "Taika's friends use racist jokes." The second idea is that the message is simply boring and a waste of time: "Lame! This'll be like the war on terror"; and part of a 'liberal' agenda: "This ad is really not good at all. In America the crazy left yell racist every time they hear something they don't like. Soon we are too afraid to say anything. Relax, chill out, share a few jokes that are not PC"; and ineffective: "Because it's really effective when people preach from a soap box." The posts in this category seemed to want Taika Waititi to be *more* of something unspecified, or less of who he is.

I Just Don't Get It!

The heavy irony the video employs, and the satire of a certain style of 'charity' advertisement, perhaps make it an uncomfortable watch, calling as it does on conscience and memories of compassion fatigue (Hoijer, 2004). Although previous research on celebrity spokespeople acknowledges the potential for resistant readings in *How Could They Get It So Wrong?*, it was unexpected that anyone might confuse the message for one supporting racism. This key concept did not engender a large number of posts (65 in total), but they occurred enough to constitute a theme.

There are no variations in *I Just Don't Get It!* The posters all reacted in a similar way, and the following post expresses the whole theme: "I don't understand what you are trying to say... we should make racism socially acceptable? I think we have seen examples of how that ends up don't you?" One or two of the posts went on to make a personal attack on Taika Waititi: "Why do you want racism to continue. I want it to stop. Some of us had enough thank you. Do you think you are white because you are famous?" In this case, the post contained not only the confusion of the writer, but also, its own seed of racism, but this type of post was in a very small minority in the theme.

I Hate, Oh How I Hate!

In this theme, we gathered together the posts (567 in total) of the people who reacted with their aggressive racism and general, often obscene, hate talk. The hatred that was expressed tended to take the form of strong but widely-diffused rage rather than a critique of a cause: the writers in this case were not engaged much with the video, but with their own visceral anger. Close to thirty contributors made more than one obscene comment, which produced a slew of angry rebuttals from other posters. An example of the posts in this group is, "Fuck the dogs. Stop the arseholes from coming, full stop, and fix our own first." Other posts were angrier, but we decided not to use them as examples because of the level of gratuitous obscenity.

This theme encapsulated a number of racist posts: "Being white is enough [to be racist]" and "Yeah, they do that ay? But....all racists love the All Blacks and when in the UK on holiday love the haka or anything Maori because they see it as THEIR culture because they don't really have a honky culture of their own (white trash)." Much of the hate talk occurred in long series of exchanges among posters:

> Sorry who gave you the right to talk smack about someone of a different colour, something you know nothing about. A life you know nothing of. If it's easy for you to be racist so easily and for the fun of it, then it

shows your privileged life. This video in fact mocks people like you yet you still try to justify your privileged life being racist.

The *ad hominem* attack quoted above is typical of the posts in this theme. It is noteworthy that abuse was sometimes directed against other posters, but was often levelled at society in general.

Racism, And Every Other Little Thing

The last theme was made up of posts that used the video as the starting point for a discussion of other, sometimes even larger philosophical matters. Of all of the themes, this was by far the smallest at 50 total posts. Posts in this category, for instance, opened up quite balanced and civil conversations about whether a particular social ill, of which racism was just one example, can ever be eradicated, leading on (for instance) to deliberations about the perfectibility of the human race. Recurrent key ideas were about notions of institutional racism and the role of the media in promoting or hindering racism.

Even when the posts were not of a widely discursive nature, they were of a sort to invite further thought and discussion:

> …I see your point but ignoring or not acknowledging the problem would mean we wouldn't have civil rights. I find it really hard to believe that turning a blind eye would have done anything for the rights of women, people of colour, children, the disabled etc. if you allow people to think there isn't a problem, then they don't do anything about it.

The posts in this theme were typically civil exchanges such as the one following, which was obviously written by two people equally exercised by the topic, but careful not to give offense: "I feel to varying degrees, racism is a human condition based on nature more than nurture," and in general, such posts earned equally civil responses: "Think about this: The more socially unacceptable it is to be racist, the more *hidden* the racism must be!" The exchange showed that some citizens are aware of and concerned about racism in New Zealand, and want to approach the topic rationally and carefully so that the problem is identified but not magnified with emotion. The effort to be objective in this theme suggested that some people took the opportunity afforded by the campaign to embark on a difficult conversation.

Discussion

Previous research (Panis & Van den Bulck, 2012; Marshall, 2013; O'Regan, 2014) showed that celebrities with a strong personal brand were likely to be selected as spokespeople for particular causes, and in the case of Taika Waititi, it does seem that the Human Rights Commission was quick to capitalise on his recent professional success and his status as the 2017 New Zealander of the year. The posts showed that Taika Waititi's signature style (Elsbach, 2009) was polarizing, confirming previous research (Garcia de los Salmones, et al., 2013; Noland, et al., 2009; Partzsch, 2015; Wheeler, 2014) that employing celebrities to be the 'face' of an issue will not guarantee universal support. The polarized responses further suggest that the message, likely did not establish a unified "imagined community" (Anderson, 1983, p. 6) that bound New Zealander's together in the meeting of a common good. In fact, although posters congratulated each other on being tolerant, open and advocates of human rights, the number of disgruntled and dissenting voices suggests that not all New Zealanders hold to these values as part of the wider New Zealand identity.

Although some posters thought the message was boring or inappropriate (Toncar, et al., 2007; Wheeler, 2014), much of the negative reaction centered on assertions that Taika Waititi's humor had itself tended to racism in his work on *Flight of the Conchords*, showing the importance of congruence between the cause and the celebrity (Toncar, et al., 2007). In this case, the disjoin between the present message and perceptions of his style of humour was too great to be overlooked, and in consequence, the message was discounted by this part of the audience because he was considered to be an inauthentic spokesperson.

Previous scholarship (Meyer & Gamson, 1995; Panis & Van den Bulck, 2012, 2014; Partzsch, 2015) warned that some celebrities avoided controversial causes or attempted to de-radicalize the message in order to avoid damage to their brand. Taika Waititi appears to have been deliberately provocative in this video, satirising another form of 'social good' message and leaning deeply into irony to make his point. A message about casual racism is in itself likely to attract comment; one in the style he chose was likely to create sensation, which, if the number and style of posts is an indicator, it did. The most basic point of a public service announcement is to raise awareness of an issue (Toncar, et al., 2007), and this video richly fulfilled that aim. At the top end, such a message must aim to change negative social behavior, or at least change attitudes towards the behavior (Petty & Cacioppo, 1984). Arguably, a radical message is the best way to proceed, because controversy, at least on social media platforms, starts conversations and by 'outing' hate talk, shows that depth of the need for social change.

Taking audience reaction from Facebook pages both widened and limited the reactions we found. On the one hand, the emotion in the platform meant that the posts can be taken as sincere, but on the other hand, they have to be seen as the immediate and probably unconsidered remarks and rejoinders that might later be dismissed by their writers. We can say that the themes we identified offer a snapshot of responses, and like all snapshots, are a summary of a moment.

Although the themes revealed both extravagant admiration for and exaggerated dislike of Taika Waititi, we saw little evidence of the parasocial relationships that might have been present, given that we were canvassing a social media platform (Basil, 1996; Cashmore, 2006). We cannot account readily in this study for the differences between the types of themes that emerged on the two different Facebook pages, but we suggest that people visit Taika Waititi's own page in forms of fan behaviour (even if the fans then expressed disappointment), while the Human Rights Commission's Page attracted people more involved in citizenship behavior. This is not to say that what we are tentatively labelling citizenship behaviour is socially desirable, but more that these people seemed much more occupied with their right, under freedom of speech, to express any opinion that they happened to hold.

Conclusion

Without doubt, public opinions on social issues change over time, and public service announcements such as "Give nothing to racism" must play a part in effecting that change. What the analysis has made clear is that 'an audience' is not a homogeneous body that reacts as a unit, but rather, is a group of individuals whose opinions coalesce around some ideas and break off into separate formations on others. In other words, no matter the worthiness of the message, and no matter the skill and craft of the rhetor, there is no way to guarantee that reception of the message will be what is sought by its designers. Since this is so, it seems that the important thing is to keep putting messages for social good before audiences, and to accept that there will initially be widely differing opinions because it is not possible to legislate for people's sentiments. It is a reasonable expectation, however, that as time passes, the range of negative expressions on a topic such as racism will moderate, and be followed, perhaps, by an alteration in behavior. Messages such as "Give nothing to racism" should continue to be made and placed before citizens to provoke powerful discussion.

References

Anderson, B. (1983). *Imagined communities: Reflections on the origin of and spread of nationalism.* London, UK: Verso.

Attride-Stirling, J. (2001). Thematic networks: an analytic tool for qualitative research. *Qualitative Research, 1*(3), 385-405.

Basil, M.D. (1996). Identification as a mediator of celebrity effects. *Journal of Broadcasting & Electronic Media, 40*(4), 478-495. doi: 10.1080/08838159609364370.

Beer, D. (2008). Making friends with Jarvis Cocker: Music culture in the context of web 2.0. *Cultural Sociology, 2*(2), 222-241.

Bennett, L. (2014). 'If we stick together we can do anything': Lady Gaga fandom, philanthropy and activism through social media. *Celebrity Studies, 5*(1/2), 138-152. doi: 10.1080/19392397.2013.813778.

Black, E. (2017, June 15). Don't let it slide: What to do when someone is racist. *Stuff.co.nz.* Retrieved June 20, 2017, from https://www.stuff.co.nz/life-style/life/93710789/dont-let-it-slide-what-to-do-when-someone-is-racist.

Boyatzis, R.E. (1998). *Transforming qualitative information: Thematic analysis and code development.* London, England, Sage.

Braun, V., & Clarke, V. (2006). Using thematic analysis in psychology. *Qualitative Research in Psychology, 3*, 77-101.

Burke, K. (1969). *A rhetoric of motives.* Los Angeles, CA: University of California Press.

Cashmore, E. (2006). *Celebrity/Culture.* New York, NY: Routledge.

Elsbach, K. D. (2009). Identity affirmation through 'signature style': A study of toy car designers. *Human relations, 62*(7), 1041-1072.

Fereday, J., & Muir-Cochrane, E. (2006). Demonstrating rigor using thematic analysis: A hybrid approach of inductive and deductive coding and theme development. *International Journal of Qualitative Methods, 5*(1), 80-92.

Garcia, de los Salmones, M.D.M, Dominguez, R., & Herrero, A. (2013). Communication using celebrities in the non-profit sector: Determinants of its effectiveness. *International Journal of Advertising: The Review of Marketing Communications, 32*(1), 101-119. doi: 10.2501/IJA-32-1-101-119.

Goodman, M.K. & Barnes, C. (2011). Star/poverty space: the making of the 'development celebrity'. *Celebrity Studies, 2*(1), 69-85. doi: 10.1080/19392397.2011.544164.

Höijer, B. (2004). The discourse of global compassion: The audience and media reporting of human suffering. *Media, Culture and Society, 26,* 4, 513—531.

Horton, D. & Wohl, R.R. (1956). Mass communication and parasocial interaction: Observations on intimacy at a distance. *Psychiatry, 19,* 215-229.

Howie, C. (2017, February 22). He's showed who and what we are to the world: Filmmaker Taika Waititi named 2017 New Zealander of the year. *The New*

Zealand Herald. Retrieved June 20, 2017, from
http://www.nzherald.co.nz/nz/news/article.cfm?c_id=1&objectid=11805601.

Hunt, E. (2017, March 20). Taika Waititi on shaking up Thor and being a Hollywood
outsider: "They take this stuff so seriously". *The Guardian.* Retrieved June 20,
2017, from https://www.theguardian.com/film/2017/mar/21/taika-waititi-on-
shaking-up-thor-and-being-a-hollywood-outsider.

Kerrigan, F., Brownlie, D., Hewer, P., & Daza-LeTouze, C. (2011). 'Spinning'
Warhol: Celebrity brand theoretics and the logic of the celebrity brand. *Journal
of Marketing Management, 27*(13/14), 1504-1524

Kogen, L. (2014). For the public good or just good publicity? Celebrity diplomacy
and the ethics of representation. *Mass Communication and Society, 18*(1), 37-57.
doi: 10.1080/15205436.2013.851699.

Lacey, A., & Luff, D. (2001). Trent Focus for research and development in primary
health care: An introduction to qualitative data analysis. Retrieved from
https://www.rds-yh.nihr.ac.uk/wp-
content/uploads/2013/05/9_Qualitative_Data_Analysis_Revision_2009.pdf

Liamputtong, P., & Ezzy, D. (2005). *Qualitative research methods*. Melbourne,
Australia: Oxford University Press.

McKee, H. (2017, February 23). Taika Waititi: 'Being New Zealander of the year
feels amazing'. *Stuff.co.nz.* Retrieved June 20, 2017, from
http://www.stuff.co.nz/entertainment/celebrities/89721931/taika-waititi-being-
new-zealander-of-the-year-feels-amazing.

Maori Television. (n.d.). Taika Waititi. Retrieved June 20, 2017, from
https://www.maoritelevision.com/taika-waititi.

Marshall, P.D. (2010). The promotion and presentation of the self: celebrity as
marker of presentational media. *Celebrity Studies, 1*(1), 35-48. doi:
10.1080/19392390903519057.

Marshall, P.D. (2013). Personifying agency: The public-persona-place-issue
continuum. *Celebrity Studies, 4*(3), 369-371. doi:
10.1080/19392397.2013.831629.

Meyer, D.S. & Gamson, J. (1995). The challenge of cultural elites: Celebrities and
social movements. *Sociological Inquiry, 65*(2), 181-206.

Newshub.co.nz. (2017, June 18). 'I thought we were a much more tolerant country'-
Dame Susan Devoy on racism. Retrieved June 20, 2017, from
http://www.newshub.co.nz/home/shows/2017/06/i-thought-we-were-a-much-
more-tolerant-country-dame-susan-devoy-on-racism.html.

NEWZEALANDONSCREEN. (n.d.). Taika Waititi: Director, actor. Retrieved June
20, 2017, from https://www.nzonscreen.com/person/taika-waititi.

Noland, C.M., Marshall, P.D., Goodale, G.G., & H.P. Schlecht. (2009). An exploration of the impact of celebrity on the HIV/AIDS pandemic. *Journal of health & mass communication, 1*(3/4), 194-210.

O'Regan, V.R. (2014). The celebrity influence: do people really care what they think. *Celebrity Studies, 5*(4), 469-483. doi: 10.1080/19392397.2014.925408.

Panis, K. & Van Den Bulck, H. (2012). Celebrities' quest for a better world: Understanding Flemish public perceptions of celebrities' societal engagement. *Javnost-the public, 19*(3), 75-92.

Panis, K. & Van Den Bulck, H. (2014). In the footsteps of Bob and Angelina: Celebrities' diverse societal engagement and its ability to attract media coverage. *Communications, 39*(1), 23-42. doi: 10.1515/commun-2014-0003.

Partzsch, L. (2015). The power of celebrities in global politics. *Celebrity Studies, 6*(2), 178-191. doi: 10.1080/19392397.2014.955120.

Petty, R.E. & Cacioppo, J.T. (1984). The effects of involvement on responses to argument quantity and quality: Central and peripheral routes to persuasion. *Journal of Personality and Social Psychology, 46*(1), 69-81. doi: 10.1037/0022-3514.46.1.69.

Preece, C. & Kerrigan, F. (2015). Multi-stakeholder brand narratives: an analysis of the   construction of artistic brands. *Journal of Marketing Management, 31*(11), 1207- 1230.

Rubin, A.M. & McHugh, M.P. (1987). Development of parasocial interaction relationship. *Journal of Broadcasting and Electronic Media, 31,* 279-292.

Stuff.co.nz. (2017, June 15). Taika Waititi tackles racism with Human Rights Commission and his brand of irony. Retrieved June 20, 2017, from https://www.stuff.co.nz/entertainment/film/93704365/taika-waititi-tackles-racism-with-human-rights-commission-and-his-brand-of-irony.

Thrall, A.T., Lollio-Fakhreddine, J., Berent, J., Donnelly, L., Herrin, W., Paquette, Z., Wenglinski, R., & Wyatt, A. (2008). Star power: Celebrity advocacy and the evolution of the public sphere. *The International Journal of Press/Politics, 13,* 362-385. doi: 10.1177/1940161208319098.

Toncar, M., Reid, J.S., & Anderson, C.E. (2007). Effective spokespersons in a public service announcement: National celebrities, local celebrities and victims. *Journal of Communication Management, 11*(3), 258-275. doi: 10.1108/13632540710780247.

Vaismoradi, M., Jones, J., Turunen, H., & Snelgrove, S. (2016). Theme development in qualitative content analysis and thematic analysis. *Journal of Nursing Education and Practice, 6*(5), 100-110.

Warhurst, L. (2017, June 15). Taika Waititi wants you to stop being 'a tiny bit racist'. *Newshub.co.nz.* Retrieved June 20, 2017, from http://www.newshub.co.nz/home/new-zealand/2017/06/taika-waititi-wants-you-stop-being-a-tiny-bit-racist.html.

Wheeler, M. (2014). The mediatization of celebrity politics through the social media. *International Journal of Digital Television, 5*(3), 221-235. doi: 10.1386/jdtv.5.3.221_1.

Part III:
Representing Gender and Nations

Michelle Obama's Political Body: Reimagining the Myth of American Womanhood

Jo Coghlan

Abstract. It matters what Michelle Obama wore. Her dressed political body is embedded with a visual code narrating new meanings about American womanhood. In how she dresses, American women can reimage the myths attached to the first lady, previously white, upper-class and elite. Hence, Obama's dressed body challenges the problematic myth of the idealization of the first lady as the symbol of American womanhood. In particular, Obama's raced body, dressed in blended fashion, affordable, cosmopolitan, utilitarian and pragmatic spoke to a generation of American women in ways just as powerful as any speech given by Barack Obama. Michelle Obama's fashion, as Friedman (2017) argues, isn't a uniform to which she conforms, rather it acts as a visual code that seeks to 'change the conversation' about American womanhood, rebranding it as ethnically and economically diverse, pragmatic and inclusive. Michelle Obama is able to do this because of her political persona and celebrity: a persona that understands the power of visual images in today's body politic.

Keywords: persona, celebrity, womanhood, first lady, Michelle Obama

Introduction

This chapter examines the political persona of former American first lady Michelle Obama (2009-2017) against the backdrop of the idea that contemporary politics is increasingly "ocular" (Green, 2009, p. 5). What this means is that today people increasingly engage with politics visually. How a political figure looks and dresses is as influential as the content of their character or their leadership ability. In some ways this is not a new concept, yet when thinking about image in terms of political persona, new ways of examining the dressed political body emerge. It is against this background of ocularity that this chapter examines the dressed political persona of Michelle Obama, and its role in reimagining American womanhood.

No persona studies have been conducted on Michelle Obama, and few persona studies have examined female political personas. What studies have been conducted on female political personas have found gendered stereotypes that act to deny agency to public women. This chapter seeks to add to a lack of persona studies on female political figures. The broader aim however is to examine the political persona of Michelle Obama via her digital self-presentations (Marshall et. al., 2015), evidenced in the visual codes that

Michelle Obama wore on her dressed political/raced body. The aim is to demonstrate that in a reading of the dressed political/raced body of Michelle Obama, there is evidence that she challenges the myths embedded in first lady discourses. In particular, Obama resists the construct of the first lady as the idealization of American womanhood: white, upper-class and elite, mothering the nation and setting the moral standards for her generation. She is able to do this because of the social capital she acquired via her political persona. In her raced body, Obama brought to the fore challenges to the discourse of the whiteness of the first lady, however, it is posited that Obama engaged in a much more complex political project.

The idea of the 'ocular' nature of contemporary politics, as noted, grounds this discussion. Central to persona studies, visual images – in this case of the dressed political body – can transcend narratives and discourse in ways not often seen as ideological. Images, especially in the digital world, have an immediate currency and are emotive. Images activate strong emotional responses which have the effect of shaping public evaluations about the character and values of public figures (Dimitrova & Bystrom, 2013). For McFarlane (2016) images act as representations or a "visual rhetoric", and in the case of the Obama's this visual rhetoric appealed to American's in "unprecedented ways" (p. 4)

In the case of Michelle Obama, it is argued that she challenges traditional understandings about the first lady, and in doing so provides a platform for American women to reimagine the notion of American womanhood. She does this via her "strategic identity" (Marshall & Henderson, 2016, p. 1) evidenced in her dressed body. Because this discussion is one of political persona, and given the importance of images to the social capital that can be gained from authentic representations of political persona, this chapter briefly contextualizes the development and consolidation of the combined image of Barack and Michelle Obamas' political persona.

Michelle Obama's initial social and political capital comes from her position as wife and mother. Only as Barack Obama's wife does Michelle Obama emerge as a political persona. The other aim of this discussion is to point to some of the strengths and weaknesses of political persona projects. This chapter then moves to the substantive issue of reading the dressed political and raced body of Michelle Obama.

Gender and Persona Studies: Finding Michelle Obama

Michelle Obama is an unusual study of political persona. Persona studies have mostly focused on male politicians with the exception of the work of Higgins and McKay (2016) and Van Zoonen (1998, 2000, 2005) who have mainly focused on European female leaders. Gaffney and Lahel (2013) have lamented the lack of female persona studies: a gap this discussion seeks to fill. In the case of the Obama's, persona studies have focused exclusively on Barack Obama. Barack Obama's political persona, for example, has been examined as charismatic discourse (Tirlea, 2016), mediated political masculinity (Smith, 2016), in narratives of national identity (Hammer, 2010) and via Redmond (2010, p. 81) and Marshall's (2014, p. xxiv) engaging idea of Barack Obama as "liquid" political celebrity.

In research conducted by Higgins and McKay (2016) they found the existence of "established gendered discourses" (p. 238) when examining female political personas. This is supported by van Zoonen (2006) who argues that the problem is that female political persona is:

> articulated primarily with the codes and conventions of media representations of women; of Hollywood conventions…[and]…popular myths of femininity: as enigmatic and threatening, as nurturing and caring…and as bodily practice. Inevitably, female celebrities will be constructed from these mythologies. (p. 291)

While there is evidence that Michelle Obama was narrated and framed within these gendered codes, conventions, practices and myths, this discussion posits that Michelle Obama was an active agent in shaping her own political persona. While celebrity and persona studies are often linked, arguably there is an agency attached to the construction and maintenance of a political persona. In the case of Michelle Obama, given she was first lady, and noting the public fascination with the role, the idea of celebrity is easily attached to Michelle Obama.[1] What is less examined is how Michelle Obama can be viewed from the lens of political persona?

Persona is embedded in the images that shape public opinions about a public or political figure. The images that inform understandings about a political figure are not traditional political tropes, such as their ability to give engaging political speeches or master complex legislation. Rather, it is a set of images

---

[1] Celebrity in this sense refers to the global brand recognition of Michelle Obama. However, Mark Wheeler (2013) provides a broad theoretical discussion of the concept of political celebrity (noting also its difference from persona) as: mediatization of a public rather than real persona (Drake & Miah, 2010); as an elite that seeks publicity (Meyer & Hinchman, 2002) or as a power elite (Mills, 1956); as an illusion (Boortsin, 1971), as a packaged product (Franklin, 2004); as "idols of production" (Lowenthal, 1944); as a means to neutralise citizen engagement (Turner, 2004), and similarly celebrity as a focus away from the complexity of politics embedded with symbolism that undermines democracy (Kellner, 2010).

that shape views about their identity. In the case of a political actor, voters make decisions about their character and values via a set of social and cultural frames that are much different from political frames (speeches, legislative ability etc.). This is noted in the seminal work of Daniel Boorstin (1961; 1971) and its development by Green (2009) and Wheeler (2013). For Wheeler (2003, p. 10) the subsuming of politics into the culture industry is problematic because politics becomes another commodity to be marketed, consumed and purchased, devaluing representative democracy. Conversely, van Elteren (2013, p. 264) argues that it is in these cultural spaces, the image-driven political celebrity is generating cultural meanings about themselves but at the same time the voter/audience is negotiating and organizing their own meanings about the political celebrity.

In thinking about political persona, the public determine reflexively the personality, character and values of the political figure. Because this transaction is occurring in non-traditional spaces, such as popular culture and social media, political communications between a political figure and the public appear less ideological than traditional political communications (campaign advertisements, for example). In these spaces a considerable amount of political and social capital can be gained by a political actor able to successfully negotiate this incongruent space. The success of this negotiation relies on understanding that politics today is about spectatorship. Jeffrey Green's concept of "ocular democracy", as noted in the introduction, is informative. He argues that people today "engage with politics primarily through their eyes, rather than their voice" (2009, p. 5). It is this grounding that informs the following brief overview of the Obamas' focus on imagery as narrative and rhetoric to build and sustain political capital.

Locating the Obama's political persona

The Obamas' arrived in American politics at time when the mass media was being disrupted by social media. Traditional media gatekeepers, and their control over political communications were supplanted by politicians themselves, increasingly seeking to control their own narratives and images (Gitlin, 1980, p. 7; Driessens, 2012, p. 648; Sternheimer, 2011, p. 8). As a result, though not for the first time, the idea of the celebrity politician took hold. While the celebrity politician risks becoming a commodity rather than a leader, successful political marketing and branding can generate enormous amounts of political and social capital that can translate into power (Zavattora, 2010, p. 123-124). Because of the nature of the new media landscape, particularly social media, images increasingly establish and maintain voter's understanding of the character and values of the political celebrity.

There is a danger in this, especially if there is an overreliance on visual images that results in politicians becoming "hyperreal simulations" (Zavattaro (2010, p. 126). For Zavattaro (2010) they risk becoming "not an actual leader, but an image of leader" or more problematically they risk becoming an "embodied image of a national brand" (p. 126). This type of commodification has negative consequences, especially for the public sphere. Postman (1987), and West and Orman (2003) argue that emphasis on personality detracts voters from the serious and substantive issues of governance and leadership because politics is trivialized. Yet, Putnam (2000) counters that celebrity politicians are finding new ways to connect with disconnected voters resulting in new forms of social capital. For Street (2004) the celebrity paradigm is reinvigorating politics by engaging more deeply with social attitudes, and with the authority they gain, politicians are better able to promote agendas that reflect popular opinion and enable aspirations.

The Frankfurt School accept the view that politics has always operated within the culture industry. Wheeler (2013) has charted the rise of celebrity politics as a phenomenon that predates late modernity. Noting the intensification of celebrity politics with the advent of mass communications, Wheeler reminds us of how American presidents came to rely on celebrity endorsements for their elections. The symbolism of celebrity fame attached itself to the candidate. The candidate in turn adopted a celebrity status that meant voters could see them in terms of their character and values in spaces that were more socially and culturally accessible. The nexus of celebrity and politics has proven a powerful and rewarding framework for political candidates, as the elections of John F. Kennedy, Ronald Reagan, Bill Clinton, Barack Obama, and Donald Trump demonstrate.

But it is the Web 2.0 campaigns, such as those of the Obamas' that sees political celebritization enter hyperreality. Extending ideas of commodification and celebritization, the Obama era of febrile "media spectacles" (Wheeler, 2013, p. 67) cultivated the Obamas' into political personas. The Obamas' actively and intuitively employed, and more so saturated, the Internet with campaign material as well as life style content about themselves and their children. Saturation-level digital campaigning is now considered a vital necessity in what is considered a permanent electoral cycle. It allows politicians to consolidate support from their voter base and gives them a platform to attract new voters (Gerodimos & Justinussen, 2015, p. 114). Xenos and Moy describe the Obamas' strategy as "a critical turning point" because it is when online politics "finally reached a mainstream audience" (2007, p. 704).

Reaching the heights of political celebrity, however, requires more than an extensive Web 2.0 strategy. For Corner (2000) the success of the political persona is that the demonstration of the claim to represent a group or cause requires authenticity. Drawing on the work of Erving Goffman (1959), Corner (2000) posits the distinctiveness of political persona because of the:

> scale of its projection (in political leaders this becomes national and possibly global), the degree of self-conscious strategy attending its planning and performance, the intensity of the interaction with media systems and the degree to which certain personal qualities are seen…to enhance…[and to] underwrite political values. (p. 387)

Usher (2016) suggests that political persona is made up of "complex performances of political identity" (p. 19) that have agency when authentically performed. If deemed authentic by audiences (noting the polysemic nature of performance), and when it goes viral because of the global reach of social media, it delivers the political persona an enormous amount of capital. Evidence of this was the power of the Obamas' in allowing and encouraging voters to join them in the potent idea that "everyone is included and that this movement is actually a conversation to which everyone is invited" (McGirt, 2008, p. 89).

For Street (2004) politicians that engage in persona politics do so using their "celebrityhood" allowing them to "establish their claim to represent a group of cause" (p. 435). In the case of the Obamas', their authenticity is grounded in their own representation as middle-class Americans who achieved the American Dream, positing it is also possible for others to do so. It is a narrative far removed from the dystopian one of the Tea Party Republicans drawing on the fear of 9/11 insecurity. It is in the authentic performance of this claim, that the Obamas' sought to be the representatives of those disenfranchised and disillusioned and more so, via their own narrative, seek to reestablish the aspirations of American voters. It is here that the narratives of the Obamas' are most evident.

Together Barack and Michelle Obama came to represent themselves, via personal narratives as "quintessentially America" (Hill Collins, 2012, p. 124). Barrack drew on narratives of a multicultural, cosmopolitan family, while Michelle drew on her slave heritage. Together as a family, they represented a rhetoric that posited they embodied the lynchpin of the American Dream: that of the 'American family'. Taken together, Hill Collins (2012) argues that the Obamas' representations signaled a "colourblindness" to race by "evoking traditionally gendered construct[s] of family" and they "recast American national identity in ways that incorporate diverse populations and experiences" particularly of the "multicultural American national family" (2012, p. 127).

The importance of this, particularly for Michelle Obama, is evident with the election of Barack Obama in November 2008, when Michelle Obama became the first African American first lady.

The American First Lady: Idealizations of American Womanhood

As the first African American first lady, Obama's raced body challenges the myth that the first lady was the idealization of American womanhood: white, upper-class and elite. Evident in Obama's dressed political body are a set of narratives about how American womanhood can be reimagined as more racially and economically diverse and hence inclusive. As such, via her political persona, predicated on her persona and celebrity, and sustained and circulated via the power of social media, Michelle Obama is a powerful visual queue for how American women can also reimagine the first lady.

Like Jacqueline Kennedy, Michelle Obama understands that fashion can act performatively to reimagine the identity of American womanhood and rebrand the first lady in modern America. Following the election of John F. Kennedy in 1961, Jacqueline Kennedy developed a style and look that actively sought to "show the world that despite its reputation of being a rustic, uncultured country, [the] United States was a nation of elegance, poise and culture" (Halbert Bond, 2012, p. 133). The power of the first lady is grounded in their celebrity as the wife of the president, and as such they hold a symbolically significant place in American culture. Yet, each first lady is required to authentically "perform" gender in ways that are socially assigned (Butler, 1990, p. 34; Cook & Hasmath, 2014, p. 977). The first lady is bound by ideas of what the 'traditional' role of the position is: wife, and ideally a mother. While it is acknowledged that the notion of "traditional roles" are evolving (Scharrer & Bissell, 2000, p. 55), research conducted by Scharrer and Bissell (2000) in fact demonstrates that first ladies are punished for operating outside of their "traditional roles" yet traditional roles remain subjective.

Made more difficult, first lady performance is done on a very public stage and it must be done in ways which conform to the "ideal" American woman (Kahl, 2009, p. 316). Gould (1985, p. 537) notes: "How we view the first lady is how we expect women to act, marriages to work, families to grow, and Americans to live. In the most profound sense…the first ladies hold up a mirror to ourselves". Hence, there are discursive expectations that first ladies perform what is pretended to be a "single universally accepted idea for US womanhood" (Kohrs Campbell & Burkholder, 1996, p. 191). This denotes that the American first lady is considered a site of authentic American womanhood (Vasby Anderson, 2004). This further suggests that there exists an ontologically authentic modern American woman (White, 2011, p. 11). Yet, the idea of there being one archetypal modern American women is one that has never existed (Kohrs Campbell, 1998, p. 15).

The female body in Western society, and especially for first ladies as the idealization of womanhood, is socially, politically and culturally constructed and understood via the dressed body. Dress is a situated bodily practice considered "fundamental to the microsocial order" (Entwistle, 2000, p. 325). The dressed body reinforces and sustains views about the wearer's identity. As a socially regulated practice the dressed female body is "heavily mediated" and becomes a symbol of its "location" in society and culture (p. 327). Clothing thus acts as a visible envelope of the self and serves as a metaphor for identity (Davis, 1992).

The dressed body then is a key site for interrogating gender performance and in this case, its articulation of the idealized identity of American womanhood (Entwistle, 2000). As Craik (1994) observes, the dressed female body is a "communicative device that speaks to observers and demands a response and a connection" (p. 5). Michelle Obama's dressed political/raced body does this in terms of reimagining modern American womanhood. This is a worthwhile project because as Carlson notes the American first lady is the "most tradition-bound and antiquated model of American womanhood' (1992, p. 31).

Reading Michelle Obama's dressed political/raced body

Michelle Obama is the first African American first lady. This is significant in terms of how she is received by the American public. As Meyers (2013) remind us: "When Michelle Obama was first introduced to the American public in 2008, she was depicted in the media as an unpatriotic, stereotypical, angry Black woman" (p. 20). Yet by 2014 a Gallup poll found her popularity had reached 72% (Brown, 2014). It is not surprising that the social media savvy Obamas' would adopt social media to challenge early negative attitudes about Michelle Obama. As Strangelove (2010) notes the Obamas' were "renowned" for their "sophisticated use of the Internet" (p. 139). For Hill Collins (2012) the early strategy is to take her media "visibility" and to package representations of her in ways that shaped social meanings about "race, gender, class…[and] nation" (p. 137-138).

Using 'family rhetoric' Michelle Obama is framed, via images, as reinterpreting the role of the first lady, racially but also domestically. That is, the traditional idea of the first lady being the hostess at the White House constructs Michelle Obama as the "public figure that advanced the agenda of the White House" (Hill Collins, 2012, p. 137-138). This is a distinct shift in advancing the idea of women from the private sphere to the public sphere. Secondly, there was a distinct shift in the representations of the first lady and mothering. Gone (or at least silenced) is the idea of Michelle Obama as the 'mother of the nation' (as attached to former first ladies). Instead the representations shifted to the idea of Michelle Obama as 'Mom-in-Chief' (a moniker of Commander-in-Chief which refers to the role of the President as a military commander). In this instance, the representation posited the ideal of mothers/women as powerful. Lastly, by representing Obama as both a stay-at-home mom and a career woman, Michelle Obama was able to blur work/family boundaries so the she could appeal to both traditionalists and feminists (Hill Collins, 2012). The shifts that Obama was framing were informed in many ways by the visual codes of her dressed body; arguably as powerful as any speech and likely just as influential.

In Michelle Obama's use of color, vivid shades, primary hues, bright and contrasting prints, and bold geometric designs, a reading of her dressed political/raced body signified and reinforced the "optimism and change" heralded in with the election of Barack Obama (Halbert Bond, 2012, p. 133). Just as her dressed body can posit feelings of optimistic change, her dressed body codes Michelle Obama as an 'everyday' women normatively performing pragmatic, utilitarian every-day American womanhood (Joseph, 2011). This is opposed to the idealized version of the first lady embedded in previous first lady discourses as white, upper class, and elite.

Evidence for this is found in Obama's decisions to wear off-the-shelf department store fashion. The wearing of affordable off-the-shelf fashion from American retailers like Target, Macy's, Neiman Marcus, J. Crew and Tracy Reece shape a narrative of Obama as being a busy, everyday mother, less concerned with fashion and appearances because of her daily demands in being a mother and wife and running the family home (all be it the White House). In her purchasing of every-day off-the-shelf fashion it posits her financial prudence (Clifford, 2008), dovetailing Barack Obama's calls for fiscal responsibility. More so, her choices of every-day off-the-rack fashion, notably her penchant for cardigans that she so often wore with the sleeves pushed to her elbow, narrated her 'can-do' attitude (which also operated in unison with Barack Obama's discourse of reform).

Insight into the power of Michelle Obama's dressed political body occurred in 2008. Following the fallout from revelations about the cost of the wardrobe of Vice-Presidential Republican candidate Sarah Palin (estimated to be US$150 000), Michelle Obama was asked about what she wearing during an interview on *The Tonight Show*. Her outfit was from J. Crew, an affordable

American online department store retailer. Wearing a US$148 pencil skirt, a US$148 tank top and a US$118 yellow cardigan, framed Michelle Obama's everydayness, pragmatism, utilitarianism and fiscal responsibility. Arguably, Obama understood the impact of her clothing, specifically selecting it as a political riposte to Palin. For Friedman it was a "strategic rethink about the use of clothes that not only helped define her tenure as first lady, but also started a conversation that went far beyond the label or look" (2017, online). It was a 'conversation' that set about disrupting the ideal of American womanhood that has historically been socially constructed within the first lady discourse.

Having said that, Obama didn't reject the high-end fashion associated with former first ladies; rather she supplemented her wearing of designer gowns with gowns designed by "hyphenated" (this is a reference to their mixed American and migrant backgrounds) American designers (Tate, 2012, p. 231; Brown, 2012, p. 248). Positing further disruptions to the idealization of American womanhood/first lady discourses as white and elite, Obama's dressed body posited that high-end and everyday fashion could be blended. Her appearance on the cover of *Vogue* magazine (2013) in an off-the-rack sweater with a formal full-length ball skirt, titled the "American Ideal", blended ideas of everyday fashion with high-end fashion as a metaphor for the coming together of women from different socio-economic backgrounds.

Further, in Obama's last public speech in 2017, she proclaims: "our diversity of faiths, colors, creeds that is not a threat to who we are: it makes us who we are" and "the proof was…on her back" (Friedman, 2017, online). In her choice of designers, mixing high-end fashion with every-day off-the-rack clothes, and with a penchant for cardigans with sleeves rolled up, what Michelle Obama wears matters. Her attire as first lady reflects what America is: a "melting pot and the establishment; the one percent and the accessible" (2017, online). Her clothes resonate this. They are an "expression to an idea" (Friedman, 2017, online). As such, in her dressed political/raced body Michelle Obama has soft power.

In these two examples from 2008 and 2017, Michelle Obama via her dressed political body is 'speaking' visually to different cohorts of American women. Polysemic meanings will always be evident when reading aspects of identity via the dressed body. Yet her cosmopolitan wardrobe of every-day off-the-rack affordable fashion with new, ethnically diverse high-end fashion designers, speaks to women from different racial and economic backgrounds and, at least visually, includes them in Barack Obama's hopeful America. But beyond that, Michelle Obama's political persona is also engaging with American women to reimagine womanhood as being more universal, ideally closing the gaps between class and race that are embedded in the idealization of American womanhood performed by previous first ladies (Tate, 2012).

This is borne out in the only qualitative study done on the impact of Michelle Obama's fashion on American women (Mathews et. al., 2015). In this study a cohort of American women suggest that Michelle Obama's fashion allow women to "be what you want to be" regardless of others' expectations (2015, p. 6), that she gave women "permission to challenge fashion norms" (p. 6), and to "represent themselves from a more diverse perspective…through the distinctive attributes of clothing (p. 8). In this study of Obama's dressed body, she is found to be "relatable" (p. 10) and "aspirational" (p. 8).

Michelle Obama's political persona also sought to reimagine and rebrand American womanhood in terms of race. The space of the first lady has been constructed aesthetically over time as an exclusive place occupied by white bodies. As an 'insider' (Barack Obama's wife), Michelle Obama is also an 'outsider' (African American). Michelle Obama's body unmasked the universal somatic norm of the first lady as white (Tate, 2012, p. 230). What Michelle Obama's body communicated is that the status of 'woman' hasn't been, or is, historically equal. The referent 'woman' in American culture has traditionally signified "white woman" (White, 2011, p. 11). With the first lady role "silently organised" around "domesticity, regality and hostessing" (2011, p. 12), Michelle Obama's presence brought to the fore the black female/white female dichotomy, which is pervaded with stereotypes of white women as White (2011) suggests:

> feminine, hidden in the domestic sphere, pure, pale, delicate,
> emotionally and physically restrained and black women as public,
> exposed, hypersexual, abnormal, degraded and bitchy. (p. 12)

Unlike her predecessors, Obama is unable to take cues from those that came before. Her elevation reminds audiences that American womanhood is a "script" that "assumes the first lady to be white" (Tate, 2012, p. 233). For Obama to overcome this she has to reimagine the national space of the first lady that is already "defined and designed around constructions of white femininity" (White, 2011, p. 11). Actively and consciously, it is argued, Michelle Obama embedded in her persona universally understood visual cues that could speak to multiple cohorts of American women, thus reimagining American womanhood into a less exclusive set of racial and social tropes.

In this instance, Michelle Obama drew on "family rhetoric" to frame self-representations. As Hill Collins (2012) states "Michelle Obama's interpretation of her status as first lady refracts the politics of race and gender through family rhetoric" (p. 137). The role of the first lady is neither constitutionally nor politically defined, meaning it is a social construct of conventions and traditions. The performance of its symbols of hostessing, mothering, and ceremonial duties are important to the president, hence they are important to the nation (Williams, 2009). What has been historically embedded in this subtext is that as a "white nation" America should have a "white, heterosexual family at its helm" and more so, that the "lady" of the house is "responsible for modeling the morals and the values of the American family" (Hill Collins, 2012, p. 137). For Michelle Obama, race complicated this subtext. Here "family rhetoric" helps make her highly visible race become invisible. She does this by drawing on the "Black Lady" trope – the "embracing of a politics of respectability" (Hill Collins, 2012, p. 137). This is particularly necessary because of the anxiety and hostility she received upon her elevation to the role of first lady because of her "spiker image" (Williams, 2009, p. 835).

The 'spiker image' is also a subtext of public uneasiness and insecurity associated with having a "Black women in the White House" – and even more directly the idea of "trash" occupying the White House (Faber McAlister, 2009, p. 311). Not surprisingly, Michelle Obama is regularly framed as a "stereotypical, angry Black woman" (Meyers & Gorman, 2017, p. 22). Drawing on 'family rhetoric' enables her to redress social anxiety. Here "strong black women representation" was "softened" and her "black female strength" is re-narrated as providing "strength in service to her husband's ambition…" (Hill Collins, 2012, p. 138). Obama engaged in a repackaging of self and in doing so reimagines the idea of the first lady as the archetypal American women. It is not suggested that Michelle Obama engaged in a post-identity project that denied her race; rather, as public women are required to do, she set about to rebrand herself and in doing so reimagines American womanhood.

As Milner (2005) suggests, Obama rebranded American womanhood as:

> performative, mobile, strategically essential, intersectional, incomplete, in process, provisional, hybrid, partial, fragmentary, fluid, transitional, transnational, cosmopolitan…and, above all, cultural (p. 541)

In creating a new, if liminal space, Michelle Obama's dressed political body provides a location for American women to reimage their own womanhood via a reshaped lens of the first lady. As such they are freed from the constraints of the limited white, elite script embedded in first lady performance and discourse. Obama allows the script to be reimagined linguistically, visually and stylistically in ways that arguably rebrand how American women see themselves. As a result, the idealization of American womanhood is no longer upper-class, elite, white and domestic; rather, American womanhood can be seen as more ethnically and economically diverse and multi-racial.

Conclusion

Liesbet van Zoonen's research provides a context to understand how Michelle Obama needs to be read in terms of her own womanhood and self-identity within the terrain of political persona and celebrity. Political women, it is noted, are framed and labelled differently to political men. Similarly, labels of celebrity and celebrity power are gendered. Van Zoonen (1998; 2000; 2005) well notes this. Van Zoonen, for example, finds that "fame" is generally masculinized as it reflects public achievements whereas "celebrity" is feminized because it is "predicated on being (in the media) rather than doing" (van Zoonen, 2006, p. 290). As such, van Zoonen argues that it is the "public-private divide on which the exclusion of women from politics has been built [which] has prevented women's achievement of fame" (2006, p. 290). Citing Kathleen Hall Jamieson (1988), van Zoonen demonstrates how, in the history of public speech, women have been actively excluded because of their discursive social positions as private persons. When women are in the public sphere, they are framed within the gendered conventions and codes of femininity, as noted in how first ladies are required to perform their roles as wives of the president.

Van Zoonen (2006) also reminds us that women in the public sphere are referenced as a "visual pleasure" for men and the "epitome of the male fetish" or for others is the endlessly reworked "virgin-whore" discourse (p. 291). In van Zoonen's analysis however, there is evidence of agency among female celebrities who are subverting "myths of femininity by explicitly playing with them and reinventing them" (p. 291). Hence, it matters what Michelle Obama wears. Arguably Michelle Obama is reinventing the narratives and discourses associated with the first lady, but more so she is active in rebranding American womanhood. As Cooper (2010) puts it, Michelle Obama has used her "public platform to expand limiting definitions of womanhood and ladyhood and to open the White House to communities of color and ordinary citizens" (p. 41). As a result, she has energized American women from different race and class backgrounds to participate in a reimagining of first lady/womanhood myths.

In this discussion of the dressed political body of Michelle Obama and its agency in reimagining American womanhood, the gendered nature of political persona comes to the fore. To consider issues of gender and persona, this chapter begins with a discussion of the consolidation of political persona and celebrity evident in the Obamas'. The aim of this is to establish a framework within which to locate Michelle Obama as a political persona. This is necessary in order to establish how in politics, the image matters. In this chapter, it has been argued that Michelle Obama's image matters because embedded in it are visual codes that allow American women to reimage the idealization of American womanhood.

As a persona study, one of the aims should be to examine both the "public self", in this case Michelle Obama, and consider the authenticity of their "everyday performance" that often occur in "highly privileged" digital cultures (Barbour et. al., 2014, online). Authenticity is important because without authenticity neither the persona, the message, or the medium will matter. The aim of persona studies is to understand how individuals "strategically assemble" their persona so as to "influence" for advantage. As such persona studies are a "character stud[y] of public figures" (Barbour et. al., 2014, online). In this sense, a case study of how the political persona of Michelle Obama sought to rebrand American womanhood, seemed apt.

As a first lady, Michelle Obama has a public persona that, by virtue of her marriage, means she has a political persona. More so, her persona is public, performative and celebritized. It is what political personas do with their public platform that has been of interest. In this case, it has been a study of the effects of Michelle Obama in challenging the myths of American womanhood and reimagining how the first lady can build a narrative of inclusion that has been of interest to this discussion.

References

Barbour, K., Marshall, P.D., and Moore, C. (2014). Persona to persona studies. *M/C Journal, 17*(3). Retrieved, December 17, 2017, from http://www.journal.media-culture.org.au/index.php/mcjournal/article/viewArticle/841.

Boorstin, D. (1961). *The image, or, what happened to the American dream*. London: Weidenfeld and Nicolson.

Boorstin, D. (1971). *The image: A guide to pseudo events in America*. New York: Atheneum.

Brown, C. (2012). Marketing Michelle: Mommy politics and post-feminism in the age of Obama. *Comparative American Studies, 10*(2-3), 239-254.

Brown. A. (2014). Michelle Obama maintains positive image. *Gallup Poll*. Retrieved from http://news.gallup.com/poll/167696/michelle-obalam-maintains-positive-image.aspx.

Butler, J. (1990). *Gender trouble: Feminism and the politics of subversion*. London: Routledge.

Carlson, M. (1992). All eyes on Hillary. *Time, 140*(11), 31-38.

Cook, J., and Hasmath, R. (2014). The discursive construction and performance of gendered identity on social media. *Current Sociology, 62*(7), 975-993.

Cooper, B. (2010). A'n't I a Lady?: Race women, Michelle Obama, and the ever-expanding democratic imagination. *Study of the Multi-Ethnic Literature of the United States (MELUS), 35*(4), 39-57.

Corner, J. (2000). Mediated persona and political culture: Dimensions of structure and process. *European Journal of Cultural Studies, 3*(3), 386-402.

Clifford, S. (2008). J. Crew benefits as Mrs. Obama wears the brand. *New York Times*. Retrieved December 17, 2017, from http://www.nytimes.com/2008/11/17/business/media/17crew.html.

Craik, J. (1994). *The face of fashion: Cultural studies in fashion.* New York: Routledge.

Drake, P., and Miah, A. (2010). The cultural politics of celebrity. *Cultural Politics: An International Journal, 6*(1), 49-64.

Davis, F. (1992). *Fashion, culture and identity.* Chicago: University of Chicago Press.

Dimitrova, D., and Bystrom, D. (2013). The effects of social media on political participation and candidate image evaluations in the 2012 Iowa Caucus. *America Behavioural Scientist, 57*(11), 1568-1583.

Driessens, O. (2012). The celebritization of society and culture: Understanding the structural dynamics of celebrity culture. *International Journal of Cultural Studies. 16*(6), 641-657.

Entwistle, J. (2000). *The fashioned body: Fashion, dress and modern society.* Cambridge: Polity.

Faber McAlister, J. (2017), _____ Trash in the White House: Michelle Obama, post-racism, and the pre-class politics of domestic style. *Communications and Critical/Cultural Studies, 6*(3), 311-315.

Franklin, C. (2004). *Packaging politics: Political communication in Britain's media democracy* (2nd ed). London: Arnold.

Friedman, V. (2017). What Michelle Obama wore and why it mattered. *The New York Times*. Retrieved, December 17, 2017, from https://www.nytimes.com/2017/01/14/fashion/michelle-obama-first-lady-fashion.html.

Gaffney, J., and Lahel, A. (2013). Political leadership persona: The UK Labour Party Conference of 2012. *Government and Opposition, 48*(4), 481-505.

Gerodimos, R., and Justinussen, J. (2015). Obama's 2012 Facebook campaign: Political communication in the age of the like button. *Journal of Information Technology & Politics*, *12*(2), 113-132.

Gitlin, T. (1980). *The whole world is watching: Mass media in the making and unmaking of the new Left.* Berkeley, LA: University of California Press.

Gould, L. (1985). Modern First Ladies in historical perspective. *Presidential Studies Quarterly, 15*(3), 532-540.

Green, J. (2009). *The eyes of the people: Democracy in an age of spectatorship.* Oxford: Oxford University Press.

Halbert Bond, A. (2012). *Michelle Obama: A biography.* Westport (US): Greenwood Press.

Hammer, S. (2010). The role of narrative in political campaigning: An analysis of speeches by Barack Obama. *National Identities, 12*(3), 269-290.

Higgins, M. and McKay, F. (2016). Gender and the development of a political persona: The case of Scottish First Minister Nicola Sturgeon. *British Politics, 11*(3), 283-300.

Hill Collins, P. (2012). Just another American story? The first Black First Family. *Qualitative Sociology, 35*, 123-141.

Joseph, R. (2011). Hope is finally making a comeback: First Lady reframed. *Communication and Critical/Cultural Studies, 4*, 56-77.

Kahl, M. (2009). First Lady Michelle Obama: Advocating for strong families. *Communications and Critical/Cultural Studies, 6*(3), 316-320.

Kellner, D. (2010). *Cinema wars: Hollywood film and politics in the Bush-Cheney era.* Oxford, UK: Wiley-Blackwell.

Lowenthal, L. (1944). The triumph of mass idols. In *Literature, popular culture and Society.* L. Lowenthal (Ed.). Palo Alto, CA: Pacific Books.

McFarlane, M. (2016). Visualizing the rhetorical presidency: Barack Obama in the situation room, *Visual Communication Quarterly, 23*(1), 3-13.

McGirt, E. (2008). The brand called Obama. *Fast Company, 124*, 85-92.

Marshall, P.D. (2014). *Celebrity and power: Fame in contemporary culture* (2nd ed.). Minneapolis (US): University of Minnesota Press.

Marshall, P.D., Moore, C. and Barbour, K. (2015). Persona as method: Exploring celebrity and the public self through persona studies. *Celebrity Studies, 6*(3), 288-305.

Marshall, P.D., and Henderson, N. (2016). Political persona 2016: An introduction. *Persona Studies, 2*(2), 1-18.

Mathews, D., Chaney, C., and Opiri, J. (2015). The Michelle Obama influence: An exploration of the first lady's fashion, style, and impact on women. *Fashion and Textiles, 2*(1), 1-12.

Meyers, M. (2013). *African American Women in the News: Gender, Race, and Class in Journalism.* New York, NY: Routledge.

Meyers, M., and Goman, C. (2017) Michelle Obama: Exploring the narrative. *Howard Journal of Communication 28*(1), 20-35.

Meyer, Y., and Hinchman, L. (2002). *Media democracy: How the media colonize politics.* Cambridge, UK: Polity.

Mills, C. W. (1956). *The power elite.* New York: Oxford University Press.

Postman, N. (1987). *Amusing ourselves to death: Public discourses in the age of show business.* London: Methuen.

Putnam, R. (2000). *Bowling alone: The collapse and revival of American community.* New York: Simon and Schuster.

Redmomd, S. (2010). Avatar Obama in the age of liquid celebrity. *Celebrity Studies, 1*(1), 81-95.

Scharrer, E. and Bissell, K. (2000). Overcoming traditional boundaries. *Women & Politics, (21)*1, 55-83.

Smith, A. (2016). Mediated political masculinities: The Commander-in-Chief vs. The New Man. *Social Semiotics, 26*(1), 94-110.

Sternheimer, K. (2011). *Celebrity culture and the American dream: Stardom and social Mobility*, New York: Routledge.

Strangelove, M. (2010). *Watching YouTube: Extraordinary videos by ordinary people.* Toronto, Canada: University of Toronto Press.

Street, J. (2004). Celebrity politicians: Popular culture and political representation. *British Journal of Politics and International Relations, 6*, 435-452.

Tate, S. (2012). Michelle Obama's arms: Race, respectability, and class privilege, *Comparative American Studies, 10*(2-3), 226-238.

Țîrlea, A. (2016). Barack Obama – The new charismatic political actor: A discourse analysis. *Journal of Education Culture and Society, 2*, 247-261.

Turner, G. (2004). *Understanding celebrity.* London: Thousand Oaks.

Usher, B. (2016). Me, You, and Us: Constructing political persona on social networks during the 2015 UK General Election. *Persona Studies, 2*(2), 19-41.

Van Elteren, M. (2013). Celebrity culture, performative politics, and the spectacle of 'Democracy" in America. *The Journal of American Culture, 34*(4), 263-283.

van Zoonen, L. (1998). Finally I have my mother Back: Male and female politicians in popular culture. *Harvard International Journal of Press/Politics, 3*(1), 48-64.

van Zoonen, L. (2000). The personalization of politics: Opportunities for women. *International Journal for Politics and Psychology, 9*(3-4), 19-35.

van Zoonen, L. (2005). *Entertaining the citizen: When politics and popular culture converge*, Boulder, CO: Rowman and Littlefield.

van Zoonen, L. (2006). The personal, the political and the popular. *European Journal of Cultural Studies, 9*(3), 287-301.

Vasby Anderson, K (2004). The First Lady: A site of "American womanhood." In *Leading ladies of the White House: Communication strategies of notable twentieth-century First Ladies*, edited by Molly Wertheimer. London: Rowman & Littlefield.

West, D., and Orman, J. (2003). *Celebrity politics.* New Jersey: Prentice Hall.

Wheeler, M. (2013). *Celebrity politics: Image and identity in contemporary political communication.* Cambridge, UK: Polity.

White, K. (2011). Michelle Obama: Redefining the (White) House house-wife. *Journal of Feminist Theory and Culture, 10*(1), 1-19.

Xenos, M., and Moy, P. (2007). Direct and differential effects of the internet on political and civic engagement. *Journal of Communication, 57*(4), 704-718.

Zavattaro, S. (2010). Brand Obama: The implications of a branded President. *Administrative Theory & Praxis, 32*(1), 123-128.

Jackie: Portrait of a First Widow

Melanie Piper

Abstract. This chapter examines the film *Jackie* (Larraín, 2016) by approaching the biopic as a character study. Like all biopics, *Jackie* re-creates the persona of a public figure using indelible pieces of cultural memory to supplement a historical narrative with a personal one. However, *Jackie*'s limited temporal and narrative focus on the days immediately following John F. Kennedy's assassination cause the film to deviate from traditional expectations of the Hollywood biopic. By unpacking how the film re-creates the historical public persona of Jackie Kennedy and renders her as a screen character with a plausible private self and stylistic subjectivity, I argue for a character-centric approach to the biopic. With this method, I aim to demonstrate the value of biopic films in considering the cultural meanings of public figures and the role of creative interpretation in the production and consumption of celebrity narratives.

Keywords: biopic, persona, character, Jackie Kennedy, American identity.

Introduction

On Valentine's Day, 1962, the American people were invited inside the White House to witness the work that First Lady Jacqueline Kennedy had done to bring the past into the present. Eventually televised on all three American broadcast networks, *A Tour of the White House with Mrs John F. Kennedy* was the result of a $2 million restoration of the White House that Kennedy had overseen during the first year of her husband's administration (O'Donnell, 2012). In 2016, filmgoers were invited inside and behind the same event through a re-creation of the televised tour in Pablo Larraín's film *Jackie*. With Natalie Portman's mimetic performance of Kennedy and the historically attentive set design and art direction, the Jackie Kennedy biopic not only brings back to life what television viewers saw in 1962, but adds the dimension of what could have happened beyond the boundaries of the TV camera's frame. In the biopic version, the audience can witness two Jackies at work, as we see the private woman preparing for her public performance, rehearsing her introduction to the television audience with her faithful friend and social secretary Nancy Tuckerman (Greta Gerwig). As well as re-presenting the televised event with Portman-as-Jackie in broadcast black-and-white, the film invites the audience to accept the behind the scenes moments in full, living color. When, at one point in the broadcast, Nancy gestures from off-camera to remind Jackie to smile, the audience can see the conscious performance of a public persona at work. It is a suggestion of what might have been a truth of the moment, but was invisible in its original, historical state.

As a biopic, Jackie can go further into moments such as these beyond simply allowing the audience to witness a re-constructed version of historical events. The White House tour is re-presented in the film in flashback, structured around an interview the former First Lady gives a week after John F. Kennedy's assassination. In the present moment of the film's narrative, Jackie reflects on the White House tour and her work behind it. In one of the film's meta-commentaries on the construction of history and even the role of the biopic itself in writing popular history and myth, Jackie tells her interviewer she wanted to invite television cameras into the White House to "share it with the American people. To impart a sense of America's greatness," because "objects and artefacts last far longer than people, and they represent important ideas in history, identity, beauty" (Larraín, 2016) This dialogue works with Jackie Kennedy's public persona as a woman of class, culture, and sophistication, while simultaneously noting that the way we have come to know her public persona is through objects and artefacts that may only communicate the idea of a person and what she represents, divorced from any sense of actual personhood.

In this chapter, through the example of *Jackie*, I propose that biopics can be a useful tool for considering how the popular imagination attempts to re-inject the person behind the persona into cultural discourse about public figures. At the same time, however, as *Jackie*'s meta-commentaries about the construction of history and national identity demonstrate, what we imagine the private self of a public figure to be is just another facet of their textual public image, another artefact that points to the idea of a celebrity and what they can represent to various publics. I begin by briefly considering how the biopic as a film genre works with both the public and private selves of its subjects in creating characters, before moving on to a more detailed look at how *Jackie* specifically depicts the multiple personas of its subject and how she negotiates her various roles as First Lady, First Widow, and a grieving, traumatized private woman. I then consider *Jackie* as an artefact in the canon of Jackie Kennedy's public image and public memory, and how the film uses its fictionalized protagonist/historical subject as a stand-in for ideas about national identity and the ways history can be (re)written in present tense.

The Biopic as Character Study

Popular critical response to *Jackie* raised variations on the theme that Larraín had made a biopic that was not quite a biopic. Reviews described the film as "eschewing standard biopic form at every turn" (Lodge, 2016), as giving the "sense that these [characters] are people, not figurines in a dutiful paint-by-numbers biopic" (Dargis, 2016), and as an exercize in meta-history, as the story Jackie weaves about her husband's legacy mirrors the construction of the biopic itself as a "manicured, zoomed-in version of a true story" (Sims, 2016). The biopic at its most fundamental level is loosely defined by George F. Custen (1992) as a film that is "minimally composed of the life, or the portion of a life, of a real person whose real name is used" (p. 6). If we take this as the broad, basic criteria for what constitutes a biopic, what accounts for the somewhat reluctant use of the term in *Jackie's* critical consideration? In studying the biopic as a film genre, Dennis Bingham (2010) argues that just the term 'biopic' evokes derision in both scholarly and critical circles, crediting this disdain to the genre's often loose treatment of historical accuracy and air of the self-important Oscar-bait project. Bingham writes that filmmakers will often go so far as to claim their stories based on the lives of real people are not biopics, as they aim for a sign of higher quality than what the term 'biopic' generally connotes (p. 10-11).

Critical response to *Jackie* such as the reviews noted above would indicate that the negative connotations surrounding the term 'biopic' are still in full effect in popular discourse, as the genre label recalls the classical format of a cradle-to-grave life story that reduces the subject and their significance to something that can be easily explained in three acts. I argue that *Jackie*, with its representation of a real historical figure that is presented in a way that claims to adhere to some degree of truth and factual accuracy, is indeed a biopic. However, *Jackie* is a biopic that could best be understood as a character study. This approach counters critical responses that attempt to disavow the film's connection to classical Hollywood biopic entirely, simply because it does not fit common conceptions of what the biopic form is, or what it does to public figures when they become screen characters. By approaching *Jackie* as an example of a character study biopic, I aim to shed light on the potential that all biopics, as creative representations of celebrities past and present, have for representing and negotiating ideas about fame, identity, and the private selves of public figures.

Before specifically looking at *Jackie* in terms of its work as a character study, it is first necessary to consider how biopics construct character by re-creating the known public self, supplemented by the creation of a plausible private self. Bingham (2010) writes that the goal of the biopic is to uncover a biographical 'truth' about its subject, rather than simply to restate the facts of their life in the form of a compressed screen narrative. There is an experiential dimension to the biopic that raw fact alone lacks, as the biopic, through the investigation of its subject, their personality, and their cultural significance, has the potential for "both artist and spectator to discover what it would be like to be this person" (Bingham, 2010, p. 10). What may be lost in the way of factual fidelity in the translation of history to the biopic form is gained in what Robert Rosenstone (2012) describes as "metaphoric truths" (p. 9), a sense of emotional authenticity generated by simulating access to historical events.

When the lives of the famous and instantly recognizable are re-created on screen, we as an audience are aware that the characterization of the biopic subject is cloaked in fictionalization. It is a necessity of the biopic form for invention, speculation, composition, and alteration to shape the re-presentation of a public figure. What the biopic can do, however, is persuade the viewer to believe that the character on screen is a plausible stand-in for what we know the real subject to be. If we suspend our disbelief, succumb to the cinematic illusion of the real, and engage with the screen version of a public figure *as if* they were the real thing, we can gain a kind of access to a public figure that is impossible without a fictional frame. Not only can we witness them in their private moments, but we can engage with the subjective experiences of the biopic subject-as-character as we would any fictional screen character. The experience of film spectatorship and the process of engaging with screen characters is shaped by our existing ideological understanding of who or what the screen character represents (Smith, 1995). When presented with the fictionalized version of a known celebrity that offers a variation on existing cultural understandings of their public image, the film spectator could potentially be left re-evaluating what they know about the actual historical figure represented in the biopic.

To adapt a public figure into a plausible screen character, the biopic must lay a foundation of known factual material. In the case of a well-known figure such as Jackie Kennedy, the instant recognition of iconic elements of the biopic subject's public image—such as costume, hair, and the actor's physical and vocal resemblance—helps to authenticate the screen representation (Vidal, 2014, p. 11). To apply Murray Smith's (1995) description of the types and stages of audience identification with screen characters, triggering the audience's memory of a public figure through their screen version allows the audience to recognize the biopic character as a character. This recognition subsequently prompts the spectator to map their pre-exiting notions and expectations about the biopic subject onto the screen version, where they may be confirmed or questioned as the film unfolds.

In addition to the instant recognition of evoking icon memory, the foundation of factual material in the biopic consists of what Steven N. Lipkin (2011) describes as "warrants" that ground a docudramatic depiction within the actuality that it represents (p. 3). Warrants of actuality can include biographical facts, re-creation of actual historical documents or footage, integration of actual material, or sequences that show the interaction of the re-created and the actual. The scene discussed in the introduction to this chapter, the re-presentation of Jackie Kennedy's 1962 White House tour, is an example of a factual warrant that grounds the film's docudramatic representation in historical reality. The televised tour is a known event, and the film's re-creation of it bears a recognizable resemblance that takes elements such as dialogue, actor blocking, and cinematography from the original. Additionally, this faithful re-creation directly interacts with clearly staged dramatic footage in the form of behind-the-scenes moments such as Jackie rehearsing her lines with Nancy before going on camera.

The biopic's foundation of factuality and integration of the audience's collective memory of the subject can be thought of as being constructed from what Richard Dyer (1987) describes as the "star image". Intertextual and transmedia material, consisting of "everything that is publicly available" about the celebrity (p. 2), can be selectively chosen by the creative stakeholders in the film—such as screenwriter, director, and actor—in order to collaboratively construct the factual basis of the biopic character. Some elements of the star image (or perhaps 'public image', to use a broader and more inclusive term that can describe a variety of celebrities who are not strictly 'stars') might be instantly recognizable through their constant cultural circulation. One example of such a widely circulated and immediately familiar image is the pink Chanel suit and matching pillbox hat Jackie Kennedy wore the day of JFK's assassination. Other chosen elements of the biopic subject's public image, such as the televised White House tour in *Jackie*, may not be as instantly recognizable (particularly, in this case, to a younger audience), but nevertheless serve to forge a connection to historical reality, as well as support the film's narrative, characterization, or thematic goals. The availability of historical information, photographs, and video online can additionally give these less-recognizable pieces of a public image a retroactive sense of accuracy to the film. This is especially that case if, for example, a viewer chose to look up the White House tour on YouTube after viewing the film in order to assess the accuracy of the film's depiction.

When considering how the factual foundation of the biopic subject aids in crafting a plausible screen character, it is useful to apply Erving Goffman's (1959/1990) dramaturgical metaphor for everyday self-performance. To simplify the basic concept of the metaphor, Goffman defines regions of behavior as front-stage, for the public presentation of self, and back-stage, where the performance is prepared but not enacted. To return to the White House tour sequence in *Jackie*, the moments before Jackie steps in front of the camera, when she is rehearsing her opening greeting with Nancy, could be considered a version of Jackie's back-stage self, extrapolated from an existing front-stage element of her public image (the actual televised White House tour itself). It is this back-stage, private self that is the work of imagination and speculation in the biopic. For the biopic to not simply be a narrative recounting of historical fact, for the film to generate some kind of emotional hook or affective connection with its story and characters, the unseen lives and inner selves of public figures need to be made visible through their screen versions. While the spectator retains the knowledge that there is a degree of invention to the back-stage or private self on screen, the recognizability and factuality laid out in re-creating the public self of the biopic subject can help to persuade the viewer that what has been invented has been done with similar degrees of accuracy. Or, if not the same fidelity to historical accuracy, the private self that has been extrapolated from the public image can at the very least persuade the viewer that there is a degree of believability and cohesion between the public and private selves as they are presented simultaneously in the biopic character.

With this merging of fact and fiction, creation and re-creation, occurring at the site of the public and private selves of a celebrity subject, the biopic character becomes the locus of the liminal truths that are the foundation of the biopic as a genre. By approaching biopics as character studies, the biopic film can potentially be used to further investigate not only cultural understandings about the public and private selves of celebrities, but how the cultural imagination becomes a factor in constructing narratives of who we want celebrities to be as private people. What occurs at the liminal boundaries of their public/private selves can then be used to represent cultural imaginations in contemporary historical narratives. *Jackie*, with its restricted narrative timeline and narrative scope, as well as the film's stylistic evocation of its protagonist's emotional subjectivity, is an apt example to approach as a character study biopic. With the foundations of how biopic characters are constructed from the known public and imagined private selves of their subjects established, I now move on to a more detailed examination of the multiple selves of Jackie Kennedy as a screen character that are deployed in *Jackie*: the re-created public, the witnessed private, and the unseen subjective.

Constructing, Reconstructing, and Deconstructing *Jackie*

According to Bingham's (2010) work on the biopic genre, biopics about women are structured around a completely different set of tropes and characteristics than their male-subject counterparts. This results in biopics about women forming their own distinct biopic sub-genre, as a cultural resistance to women in the public sphere sees them depicted on screen through "myths of suffering, victimization, and failure" (Bingham, 2010, p. 10).

Bingham notes, however, that a conscious application of a feminist point of view can steer biopics about women away from these tropes (p. 10). Jackie Kennedy's place in the public eye was dependent upon her husband's power, and the fact of his assassination has the potential for her life to be narrativized in terms of these myths of suffering. In *Jackie*, however, her subjectivity is foregrounded, and she is given agency over the chaos of tragedy as she works to control the Kennedy myth. In depicting Jackie's private work in constructing the Kennedys' public persona, the film offsets its intimate depiction of Jackie-as-victim by representing a woman consciously working to (re)create her public and private identities.

Jackie takes a long-standing structural cue from male-subject biopics, using the investigatory device of the interview. The investigatory narrative device in the biopic is something that can be traced back to a biographical film that was technically not a biopic: *Citizen Kane* (Welles, 1941) and its search for the meaning of "Rosebud", the final words of its William Randolph Hearst-esque protagonist (Bingham, 2010, p. 19). The structuring interview weaved throughout *Jackie* is based on Theodore H. White's interview with Kennedy for *LIFE* magazine shortly after JFK's assassination (Rothman, 2016). *Jackie*'s interviewer is not identified as White, either in the dialogue of the film or in the film's credits, where actor Billy Crudup's character is anonymously named as 'The Journalist'. By not strictly claiming this to be the exact conversation that took place between Kennedy and White, there is a degree of plausible deniability to its fictionalisation: this is a sense of what may have existed behind a real historical document (White's *LIFE* article), but the film does not forward the claim of it being a re-enactment. Anchored by the investigatory device of the interview taking place in the film's present tense, one week after JFK's assassination, the film moves in and out of flashbacks in response to the journalist's questions and Jackie's answers. The result is a non-linear and temporally inconsistent journey through Jackie's memories; of the glory days of Camelot; of her husband's death; the immediate aftermath, the fact of her sudden change in status from First Lady to First Widow; and her working through of this new identity as both a public and private person. To begin looking at the characterisation of Jackie Kennedy and the ideas *Jackie* uses her public and private selves to represent, I will first examine how the character is grounded in the textual factuality of Kennedy's public persona and public image. Here I will first be using the sequence depicting the Kennedys' arrival in Dallas on November 22, 1963, as an illustrative example.

Jackie is guided into this flashback when she dryly notes that she knows that the journalist is looking for a sensationalist, moment-by-moment account of her husband's assassination rather than any concrete truth, or the story that Jackie herself wishes to tell. Once again, there is a moment of Jackie preparing behind the scenes for a known part of the actual historical Kennedy public image. On Air Force One, she rehearses a speech in Spanish to the mirror as she finishes getting ready. The pink Chanel suit is already in place as she affixes the pillbox hat, the iconic image complete. She meets Jack at the door of the plane, and as the two begin to step out, the film cuts to actual newsreel footage of the Kennedys descending the stairs of Air Force One at Dallas Love Field in 1962. The long shot cuts back to a closer framing, returning to Portman-as-Jackie as she finishes the descent, shot in 16mm film to be more seamlessly intercut with the historical footage. This direct interaction of actual and re-staged footage is an example of the docudramatic warrants that Lipkin (2011) describes. The persuasive technique asks its audience to accept what we see of Portman in close up to be a continuation of what we see of the actual Kennedy in long shot, the former claiming to be a plausible depiction of what history was unable to record, as both are sewn together in temporal continuity.

The claim that the film shows what history's cameras could not capture continues as we see the Kennedys greeting people and shaking hands on the airfield rope line. Once again, it is an actual event. Here, however, the camera is positioned to capture Jackie's face in the moments when she turns away from the crowd, the opposite point of view to the newsreel cameras that were present at the actual event. Portman's performance, the tight framing on her face, and the absence of all sound from the story world, swallowed up by the sweetly haunting notes of Mica Levi's score, broadcasts a sense of Jackie's apprehension and anxiety in the moments when she turns away from the crowd. The film audience can see that she is clearly not comfortable in this moment. But before she turns to face the crowd again, her smile is back in place, public persona and private emotion demarcated and contained from the view of the American people.

The sense of the biopic audience being able to witness the unseen moments that history cannot document continues in sequences that show Jackie completely alone and unobserved. Particularly notable is a montage that seems to take place the day following the assassination. While trying to choose a place to bury Jack at Arlington National Cemetery, Robert Kennedy (Peter Saarsgard) tells Jackie that Lyndon Johnson wants to start his presidency and move into the Oval Office, and admonishes her for planning a public foot procession for Jack's funeral due to the potential security risk. Jackie responds that it is their "last chance" and that they must march with him. Alone in the White House residence that night, it seems to sink in that her last chance is also dawning, that she is being removed from both her public office and her private residence. The foregrounding of Jackie's work restoring the White House during the Kennedys' first year in office makes it clearly apparent that the intersection of her public role and private domicile is central to her identity as First Lady.

In the montage sequence, Jackie smokes cigarettes and drinks vodka and wine as she shakily raids her closets and dresses herself in the tangible fragments of her public self-as-fashion-icon. Set to Richard Burton singing *Camelot* on the record player, Jackie prowls the rooms of the White House in formal wear and cocktail dresses; gets snagged in her jewelry and gloves; gathers up photographs and pill bottles and fabric swatches; and performs the duties of a hostess for a phantom dinner party. It is not only the grief of witnessing her husband's death that has struck her, but the loss of her own identity as First Lady of the United States. In her grief, amidst the disruption of her public identity, she frantically attempts to dress herself up in it again, to perform that self again. She attempts to cloak herself in what the world knows her to be, while the truth of the fact that she is no longer sure of her place in the world, is contained within the private space of 'the People's House'. It is only through the access of the fictional frame that we can witness a version of Jackie Kennedy going through this process of grieving not only for herself and her children at the loss of her husband, but grieving for herself at the loss of her self-knowledge. While the spectator is aware that there is likely no historical record to support the factuality of this sequence, it is still a plausible enough version of what might have happened to imagine the traumatized Jackie Kennedy responding to her husband's death in a way that seems so at odds with her polished, put-together, and restrained public image.

As well as accessing the private life of a public figure by witnessing undocumented moments, the biopic can give an experiential sense of the biopic subject's life by representing their subjectivity on screen. *Jackie*'s investigatory interview device, non-linear flashback structure, and the lack of a clear classical Hollywood narrative allows much of the film to be represented as Jackie's memory. Sequences that fall in the immediate aftermath of the assassination, with Jackie on the flight from Dallas back to Washington, DC, and then at Bethesda Naval Hospital while JFK's autopsy is conducted, are an example of the film's stylistic depiction of Jackie's shattered subjectivity. These sequences are presented in fragmented vignettes, mimicking the short-term memory loss of a major trauma. We see Jackie on Air Force One attempting to regain control of the situation, asking for information on the caliber of the bullet before switching to preliminary plans for the funeral. The President's staff attempt to quiet her, to placate her, as the fractured editing leaves large, abrupt gaps in time without any logic or sense to be made. Throughout these sequences, dialogue is often cut mid-sentence, leaving many of Jackie's questions unanswered, rendering the details unimportant and her search for control unresolved.

The arrival of Robert Kennedy when they reach Washington appears to anchor her for a moment, the sudden temporal gaps suspended until the sequence reaches Bethesda. She wanders the halls of the hospital, untethered, television news playing in the background, her concerns jumping from wanting to make sure Jack will look like himself after the autopsy to the whereabouts of her children. Once again, the answers to her questions are rendered forgotten or unimportant: she asks what the children know, the answer lost in a cut to a brief flash of her and Bobby gathered around the television, before another cut and she is told to rest and is given a pill. She bounces between speculating on who the assassin is, to charging down the hall to see her husband. Bobby catches up to her and pulls her away as she sobs, already having seen too much. It is on the ride back to the White House where unobtrusive continuity editing resumes and Jackie appears to become somewhat tethered again, as she starts to consider Lincoln's funeral as an appropriate model for her husband's. John F. Kennedy will not become another Garfield or McKinley: he will be remembered. This purpose gives some order to Jackie's thoughts and formations of memory, with the fragmented editing style resuming at later points in the film when she appears to be overcome by grief and a loss of control.

It is the framing interview scenes which illustrate how Jackie has begun to regain control of herself by controlling the narrative. These scenes show Jackie managing her public and private persona in tandem, reminding the journalist that he will not publish anything without her permission, allowing her to write history in present tense and have the last word on what her husband should mean to the American people. In one interview scene, Jackie breaks down in tears as she describes the fatal shot, her surprise that the skull was flesh-colored, not white, her attempts to hold Jack's head together and the beauty she saw in him even as she knew he was dead. After a pause, she takes a drag on a cigarette and admonishes the journalist: "Don't think for one second I'm going to let you publish that. Do you understand?" (Larraín, 2016). The journalist complies. Throughout the framing interview scenes, *Jackie* offers a meta-commentary on the formation of history and myth and the idea that sometimes stories have more value than the truth does. Jackie herself acknowledges her status as an unreliable narrator of the Kennedy myth. Woven throughout the interview and flashback scenes are fragments of her conversation with a priest (John Hurt), where she acknowledges her husband's flaws, such as his infidelity. She confides that although she has been telling people she doesn't remember much of the assassination, she remembers everything. We see again scenes from the assassination, in clearer detail than the fragmented memories of earlier in the film, intercut with Jackie in her mourning veil and a voiceover declaring the guilt she feels, and that she wanted to be killed during Jack's funeral procession in order to atone.

These stark contrasts between the various roles of Jackie's private life (mother, somewhat estranged wife, grieving widow, woman who has to reassess her identity in the wake of leaving her home and her professional position) and her public solidification of the Camelot myth speak to what the actual Jackie Kennedy's role in American culture was at this pivotal historical moment. In representing Jackie's struggle with and eventual deliberate control over her public and private selves, her role as the grieving figurehead of a national tragedy makes her story one that aligns with the American myth of individualism and self-creation. As "a nation allegedly founded on ideas rather than culture or ancestry" (Schildkraut, 2014, p. 422), the United States of America is culturally in step with Jackie's declaration that objects and artefacts and the ideas that they represent are more historically sustainable than the people at their source. As the figurehead for the nation at this particular historical (and narrative) moment of tragedy, Jackie's reassessment of her own identity becomes a quest for setting the tone for the American identity in the wake of the President's assassination. The meta-historical commentary at the heart of *Jackie*'s character study is a statement on how public figures construct themselves, and how public figures who also serve as cultural touchstones and leaders of national public discourse construct themselves, their nation, and their historical moment.

At one point in her interview, Jackie rhetorically asks the journalist, "When something is written down, does that make it true?" (Larraín, 2016). By solidifying the Kennedy myth in her orchestration of JFK's funeral and her reinforcement of the glory days of the Camelot narrative in her *LIFE* interview, Jackie wills her public identity—and, in turn, the Kennedy identity and the national identity of the Kennedy era—into being. Written down and removed from the people they are in private, the Kennedys become objects and artefacts. They stand for ideas about "a rebirth of hope, a promise of youthful possibilities, and of individual commitment to create a better world" (Felkins & Goldman, 1993, p. 449). Jackie solidifies this myth, and through the lens of the biopic we are given simulated access to her public and private selves to witness this myth being made. Witnessing the public self in the guise of a cohesive character whose subjective experience we also experience, the deliberate process of creation at work in bridging the divides between public and private personas is made starkly visible. As Jackie serves as a stand-in for the American ideal, underneath the glory and glamour of the tale she tells, the nation is broken a series of disjointed, unreliable, and incomplete memories, unsure of how to be its true self or what that true self is, constantly rewriting its past in order to have a future.

Conclusion

One notable feature of Natalie Portman's performance mentioned in popular response to the film was her voice (Abad-Santos, 2017; Sunderland, 2016). Breathy, over-enunciated, an unfamiliar accent that sounded nothing like that more recognizable Kennedy Massachusetts twang. How accurate was it? Why did it sound so odd? To contemporary audiences, Jacqueline Kennedy's voice has largely been omitted from the collective memory, her image reduced to a silent artefact: the photograph of a woman in a blood-stained Chanel suit. Portman's Jackie was the first chance many viewers got to hear Jackie Kennedy speak. As the film asks its audience to consider how history is written, and how public perceptions are constructed, it also writes its own notes in the margins of Jackie Kennedy's biography. By giving a voice back to the silent iconic image, the film gives the impression of granting Kennedy her agency once again, reviving her for a contemporary audience, making the image come to life with a sense of the real person who has been lost to history. Here the story of how she rewrote herself and the Kennedy legacy is put into sound and motion, claiming truth that is only visible under the cloak of fiction.

Perhaps *Jackie* is seen as an anomaly in the biopic genre because the film does not attempt to explain its subject, or even propose that a public life can be explained or completely understood. Not only does the film present multiple public versions of Jackie—the actual, the re-created, the First Lady, the First Widow—but multiple private versions as well. Jackie is a wife, a mother, and a grieving woman whose identity is shattered by the assassin's bullet that necessitated her removal not only from her public office, but from the private space of her home. All that can really be understood about Jackie is a sympathetic response to her loss and the public pressure she faced, with conflicting demands pulling at all aspects of her life. Whether her role in solidifying the Kennedy Camelot myth in the days after JFK's assassination is seen as cynical and opportunistic, or as an admirable show of personal strength and historical foresight is ultimately up to each individual viewer's response to the film and the foundation of history it was built on. One of the features of character study biopics is what they themselves can add to cultural discourse about a public figure as such films enter the canon of an individual's star image. Open to interpretation and debate, biopics that do not follow a classical narrative or direct their audiences on how to feel about their subjects offer a valuable avenue of investigation into the role of imagination in celebrity culture. Approaching biopics as character studies can potentially shed light on what speculating about the inner, unrevealed private selves of public figures can say about who we want our public figures to 'truly' be at their core. When understanding biopic subjects as characters, the imaginative engagement with the public personas of the famous becomes the focus of the genre, allowing the consideration of how we, their publics, create different versions of who they might be and what they might mean to us as individuals, nations, and cultures.

Acknowledgments

Thank you to Lisa Bode for the guest lecture opportunity where I first started trying to put my many, many thoughts about this film on paper, and to the CMCS conference attendees in Perth for their feedback.

References

Abad-Santos, A. (2017, February). Jackie Kennedy's strange, elegant accent explained by linguists. *Vox*. Retrieved December 22, 2017, from https://www.vox.com/culture/2017/2/7/14442410/jackie-kennedy-accent-natalie-portman.

Bingham, D. (2010). *Whose lives are they anyway?: The biopic as contemporary film genre*. New Brunswick: Rutgers University Press.

Custen, G. F. (1992). *Bio/pics: How Hollywood constructed public history*. New Brunswick: Rutgers University Press.

Dargis, M. (2016, December). *Jackie*: Under the widow's weeds, a myth marketer. *The New York Times*. Retrieved December 22, 2017, from https://www.nytimes.com/2016/12/01/movies/jackie-review-natalie-portman.html.

Dyer, R. (1987). *Heavenly bodies: Film stars and society*. Houndmills: MacMillan.

Felkins, P. K., & Goldman, I. (1993). Political myth as subjective narrative: Some interpretations and understandings of John F. Kennedy. *Political Psychology, 14(3)*, 447-467. http://www.jstor.org/stable/3791707.

Goffman, E. (1990). *The presentation of self in everyday life*. London: Penguin. (Original work published 1959).

Larraín, J., Aronofsky, D., Liddell, M., Franklin, S., Handel, A. (Producers) & Larraín, P. (Director). (2016). *Jackie* [Motion Picture]. United States: Fox Searchlight.

Lipkin, S. N. (2011). *Docudrama performs the past: Arenas of argument in films based on true stories*. Newcastle upon Tyne: Cambridge Scholars.

Lodge, G. (2016, September). Film review: *Jackie. Variety*. Retrieved December 22, 2017, from http://variety.com/2016/film/reviews/jackie-review-natalie-portman-1201853716/.

O'Donnell, N. (2012, February). Jackie Kennedy's Devotion to the White House Revealed. *CBS News*. Retrieved December 22, 2017, from https://www.cbsnews.com/news/jackie-kennedys-devotion-to-white-house-revealed/.

Rosenstone, R. (2012). *History on film / film on history* (2nd ed.). Harlow: Pearson.

Rothman, L. (2016, December). This is the real *Jackie* interview with *LIFE* magazine. *Time*. Retrieved December 22, 2017, from http://time.com/4581380/jackie-movie-life-magazine/.

Schildkraut, D. J. (2014). Boundaries of American identity: Evolving understandings of "Us". *Annual Review of Political Science 17*, 441-460. DOI: 10.1146/annurev-polisci-080812-144642.

Sims, D. (2016, December). *Jackie* enters a First Lady's worst nightmare. *The Atlantic*. Retrieved December 22, 2017, from https://www.theatlantic.com/entertainment/archive/2016/12/jackie-movie-review-natalie-portman/509264/.

Smith, M. (1995). *Engaging characters: Fiction, emotion, and the cinema*. Oxford: Oxford University Press.

Sunderland, M. (2016, November). Experts explain Natalie Portman's weird voice in the new Jackie O biopic. *Vice*. Retrieved December 22, 2017, from https://broadly.vice.com/en_us/article/gyxbz9/voice-experts-explain-how-realistic-jackie-natalie-portman-voice.

Vidal, B. (2014). The biopic and its critical contexts [Introduction]. In T. Brown & B. Vidal (Eds.), *The biopic in contemporary film culture* (pp. 1-32). London: Routledge.

Transgression and Recuperation: Cary Grant, Male Stardom and the American Dream

Belinda Glynn

Abstract. Tall, dark and handsome, Cary Grant personifies classical Hollywood's perfect romantic hero. As one of Hollywood's most enduring stars, Grant's image in popular culture is so consistently represented as charming, elegant and romantic that it has almost become monosemic; however, this popular understanding of Grant misrepresents the complexities and transgressions associated with his star text. In this paper, I contend that Grant's early star persona disrupted dominant definitions of acceptable masculinity, bringing a playfulness and ambiguity to the films in which he starred and his star text more generally. Using archival research, this chapter demonstrates how when Grant first achieved stardom in the late 1930s as an actor in screwball comedies, he was more closely aligned with non-traditional masculinity than elegance and sophistication. This gender difference was also evident in the relationship between Grant and the concepts of beauty, spectacle and the gaze in his films, with him frequently being positioned in the same way as his female co-stars. However, despite the ability of his star text to play with gender norms, he avoided being feminized or punished for being transgressive. I argue that this was possible because the transgressiveness associated with non-traditional masculinity was recuperated through the constant association of Grant with American national identity. Through the narrative of being an immigrant who rose from poverty to wealth due to hard work and business acumen, Grant became a symbol of the American Dream. The alignment of Grant with the classical American success story coexisted with his gender ambiguity, resulting in a unique classical Hollywood star and a fascinating star text.

Keywords: Cary Grant, national identity, stardom, masculinity, transgression

Introduction

Cary Grant is one of studio-era Hollywood's biggest and most enduring stars. He achieved amazing success over the course of his 35-year career, consistently appearing in popular movies, many of which maintain their appeal today. Grant still circulates in popular culture as an iconic representation of the ideal tall, dark and handsome man; possessing a timeless elegance that is always perfectly in style. Richard Torregrossa describes him as "the consummate leading man, loved by women, admired by men—a star whose style is timeless, as appealing today as it was back in Hollywood's golden era" (2006, p. xii). In addition to his reputation for style, Grant is also associated with romance and charm. Pauline Kael calls him "The Man From Dream City," while Roger Ebert writes, "Everyone knows that Cary Grant was the most charming man in the movies."

However, although Grant's image in popular culture is so consistently represented as charming, elegant and romantic that it has almost become monosemic, his star persona is far more complex than the "charming man" "everyone knows." Born Archie Leach to a working-class family in Bristol, England before moving to America as part of a vaudeville troupe, 'Cary Grant' only came into being at Paramount Studios in 1932. When Grant first achieved stardom as an actor in screwball comedies, his persona was more closely aligned with non-traditional masculinity than elegance and sophistication. Over the course of his career, his star persona played with mainstream definitions of masculinity with a number of different character types, including the romantic leading man he is so frequently remembered for today.

Despite the continued public interest in Cary Grant, there has been very little academic work that critically examines this popular, much-loved actor. In this chapter, it is argued that Grant's early star persona disrupted dominant definitions of acceptable masculinity. Through the examination of archival material such as fan magazines, this chapter explores how his persona played with gender norms, representing an ambiguity concerning dominant definitions of acceptable masculinity. However, despite the ability of his star text to play with gender norms, he avoided being feminized or punished for being transgressive. This chapter argues that this was possible because the transgressiveness associated with non-traditional masculinity was recuperated through the constant association of Grant with American national identity. In particular, as an Englishman who emigrated to America and achieved great success, Grant represented living proof of the American Dream: that anyone can succeed if they just work hard enough.

Becoming Cary Grant

Born Archibald Alexander Leach to a poor family in Bristol, England in 1906, Cary Grant ran away from home as a teenager to join a vaudeville troupe, Bob Pender's stage performers (Eliot, 2004). When the group toured New York, Archie went with them. When they returned to England, he stayed behind and began to work on Broadway, with limited success. In 1931, at the age of 27, he moved to Hollywood and was signed by Paramount Studios on a five-year contract for the then-considerable sum of $450 a week (Eliot, 2004). Paramount renamed him 'Cary Grant' (the Cary coming from a character he had played on Broadway and the Grant picked at random from a list) and he began an extensive process of transformation, changing his gait, speech and attire (Eliot, 2004). These changes were the first step in the process of becoming Cary Grant. The second step was developing a consistent and individual star persona that resonated with audiences. For Grant, that step took much longer.

Grant was worked hard by Paramount, featuring in prominent roles in 26 movies between 1932 and 1937. These roles varied in type, including a wealthy playboy in *Blonde Venus* (Josef von Sternberg, 1932) and *Hot Saturday* (William A. Seiter, 1932), a reformed gangster in *Gambling Ship* (Louis J. Gasnier and Max Marcin, 1933), a detective in *Big Brown Eyes* (Raoul Walsh, 1936) and, a bit closer to his roots, an English vaudeville performer/conman in *Sylvia Scarlett* (George Cukor, 1935). This follows the process described by Tino Balio, in which a studio would cast an actor in a series of roles and test audience response through fan mail, reviews and the box office. He writes: "In essence, producers attempted to mold their protégés to fit consumer interest. Once the correct formula was found, the ingredients would be inscribed in narratives, publicity, and advertising" (1995, p. 164). However, although Grant received largely favorable reviews in these films, Paramount was unable to determine the type of role or persona that best suited his specific talents. To borrow Balio's phrase, they were unable to establish "the correct formula." As he neared the end of his five-year contract, Grant found himself repeatedly cast in roles as one-dimensional romantic leads, what Virginia T. Lane describes as "Leading Man, formula A" (1938, p. 22). Although Paramount did offer him a contract on a higher salary, Grant decided to go freelance, a decision that was unusual for stars at that time.

In order to explain why the decision to go freelance was so significant, it is necessary to look at the labor system in which Grant was working. In the star system of the classical era, actors were signed to studios on contracts of up to seven years. These contracts gave the studios immense control over 'their' actors, giving the majors the ability to decide how many and what type of movies an actor performed in each year. This control extended to the actor's personal life and (as occurred with Archie Leach) studios would commonly 'transform' actors after signing them, providing them new names, histories and hobbies. In the star system, the studios held the balance of power; for example, they could cancel contracts but stars could not. Management were able to loan performers out to other studios without the consent of the actor and, if an actor refused to be loaned to another studio or perform in any of their selected roles, they could be suspended without pay and the period of their suspension added to the end of the contract (Maltby, 2003; McDonald, 2000). However, as stars grew in popularity, so did their ability to negotiate for increases in salary and opinions about the types of roles they were cast in, often resulting in a power struggle between the star and studio (Maltby, 2003). By choosing to work as a freelance rather than contracted actor, Grant operated outside the established system for stars and was thus able to gain an unusual amount of control over not only the roles in the films he worked in but in the construction of his star persona. Effectively, by going freelance, he was able to take an active role in the construction of Cary Grant.

Going freelance was a risky move for Cary Grant. At that time, there were very few other actors who were working freelance. Only a small number of stars sought independence by working with independent producers, signing non-option or non-exclusive contracts, making a limited number of films or negotiating for a percentage of the profits (Carman, 2008). Emily Carman argues that going freelance was really only a possibility once an actor had achieved a significant box office draw that would keep them in demand. Although Grant was popular and well received, he had yet to discover the type or persona that struck a chord with audiences, so going freelance meant possibly being unable to find work, with studios more inclined to use actors on the payroll than pay extra for additional talent. The risk, however, paid off and soon after going freelance he had great success as a charming ghost in *Topper* (Norman Z. McLeod, 1937). Grant's success in *Topper* not only demonstrated that he could be a box office draw, it was with this film that Grant's persona began to consolidate and a number of stylistic, visual and performative aspects began to be associated with 'Cary Grant'. The coherent star image that had not developed while Grant was under contract to Paramount emerged in this freelance period.

Topper was followed quickly by three more screwball films: *The Awful Truth* (Leo McCarey, 1937), *Bringing Up Baby* (Howard Hawks, 1938) and *Holiday* (George Cukor, 1938). In each of these films, many of the performative and narrative elements introduced in *Topper* are repeated, thus firming his association with a particular type and assisting in the coalescence of the Cary Grant persona. In *The Awful Truth*, he plays Jerry Warriner, a man who divorces his wife after he suspects her of cheating but with whom he still shares custody of their dog, Mr. Smith. In *Bringing Up Baby*, he plays paleontologist David Huxley, who is enticed into madcap antics chasing a tiger called Baby by Katharine Hepburn's Susan Vance. In *Holiday*, he plays earnest young businessman Johnny Case, who has made money so he can go on the titular holiday and discover what life is really about. The success of these films further solidified the association of Grant with screwball comedy, an association, which only became firmer as he appeared in more comedies in 1940: *His Girl Friday* (Howard Hawks), *My Favorite Wife* (Garson Kanin) and *The Philadelphia Story* (George Cukor).

As well as repeated narrative and stylistic elements, between 1936 and 1940 Grant developed a distinctive physicality to his performance that continued to be repeated throughout his career. Grant frequently showcases his excellent physical dexterity, jumping and falling with practiced skill. In some films, this display had a narrative reason; for example, in *Holiday*, Johnny Case (Grant) and Linda Vance (Katharine Hepburn) perform acrobatics in the playroom. Grant is also frequently seen playing the piano, singing, dancing – performing, as one would expect of a trained vaudevillian. Often Grant's performance is part of the humor of the film, such as in a scene in *The Awful Truth*. Jerry Warriner thinks he will find his ex-wife Lucy (Irene Dunne) cavorting with her music teacher but instead finds her in the middle of a singing performance. He sits at the back of the room and gets tangled in his chair before falling off it completely. In addition to using the skills developed through years of working in vaudeville, other performative commonalities include doing a double-take, looking up from under a hat and grinning in delight, and an impressive verbal dexterity (Tim Palmer (2008) states Grant could speak at a speed of up to five words per second). Not all of these elements appeared in every film, but they all formed part of the star generic syntax that made up Cary Grant.

One narrative commonality with these films was the explicit presentation of Grant as an object of visual pleasure and desire. In her famous essay "Visual Pleasure and Narrative Cinema," Laura Mulvey writes:

> In a world ordered by sexual imbalance, pleasure in looking has been split between active/male and passive/female. The determining male gaze projects its phantasy on to the female form which is styled accordingly. In their traditional   exhibitionist role women are simultaneously looked at and displayed, with their appearance coded for strong visual and erotic impact so that they can be said to   connote 'to-be-looked-at-ness. (1992, p. 750)

For Mulvey, an active/passive division of labor also controls the narrative. The male figure cannot, she says, "bear the burden of sexual objectification," therefore, strategies are called into play to prevent this happening by structuring films around a main controlling figure with whom the audience can identify. The power of the male protagonist to make things happen within the story combines with the erotic power of his gaze at the female to create a satisfying sense of omnipotence. Mulvey specifically mentions male stars, but argues that rather than existing as an erotic object of the gaze, their "glamorous characteristics" work as a screen surrogate for the spectator (p. 751).

There are frequent moments in the films Grant made in this period that violate   Mulvey's   gendered   binary   of   men/active/looking, female/passive/looked at. The most obvious is the one mentioned previously, where Grant's characters perform in the diegesis. Mulvey argues that women function on two levels within narrative cinema: as an erotic object for the characters within what Mulvey calls "the screen story" (the diegesis) and as an erotic object for the spectator. When the woman performs, for example as a showgirl, these two looks are aligned and "for a moment, the sexual impact of the performing woman takes the film into a no-man's-land outside its own time and space" (p. 751). This raises the question of whether Grant's performances 'flip' this function, such that Grant takes up the position as 'showgirl' and becomes erotic object for the characters and the audience. However, Grant's in-film performances, while working primarily to showcase Grant's talent and often performing no direct narrative function (as when he drunkenly yet tunefully sings in *Topper*, for example), do not work in the same way as Mulvey's showgirl because the eroticization of the gaze is lacking. His fully clothed body in performance works in a different way to the fetishized fragmentation of Marlene Dietrich's legs or Greta Garbo's face. When he performs acrobatics in *Holiday*, we are invited to appreciate and enjoy his skill and elite physical control along with the diegetic audience; rather than performance pausing the narrative to focus on the sexual impact of Grant's body, it instead draws attention to its power and control.

Yet, Grant is undeniably positioned as an object of visual desire for female characters within his movies. He frequently appears without his shirt on for the flimsiest of narrative reasons, such as in *Bringing Up Baby*, where he is shown in the shower and, although Susan has a shower at the same time, there is no similar shot for her. His looks are constantly being remarked upon within the diegesis. Upon returning home from a seven-year absence in *My Favorite Wife*, Ellen's (Irene Dunne's) first question is "Is Nicky [her husband, played by Grant] as handsome as ever?" (The answer is, of course, yes). In *In Name Only* (John Cromwell, 1939), Suzanne (Helen Vinson), the best friend of Grant's character Alec's wife Maida (Kay Francis), pursues him constantly and unashamedly and, near the end of the film, attempts to blackmail him into having an affair with her (at one stage she purrs, "If the cat will play, why won't the cat play with me?").

As well as being vocally desired within the narrative, it is noteworthy how often Grant is used as a spectacle in these films. Of women as spectacle, Mulvey writes: "Her visual presence tends to work against the development of a story line, to freeze the flow of action in moments of erotic contemplation" (p. 750). Grant's films are littered with moments where the narrative pauses in erotic contemplation of his body. In *Bringing Up Baby*, Susan is so entranced by seeing Grant's face without glasses she enters an almost literal trance. When he startles her out of her reverie, she remarks, "You are so handsome without your glasses." Alternately, when Hepburn's Tracy is explaining why she left Grant's C.K. Dexter Haven in *The Philadelphia Story*, she says, "It [drinking] made you so *unattractive*," again focusing on Grant's visual appeal. Susan's comment further supports the alignment of Grant with the feminine, recalling

Mary Ann Doane's observation that the woman who wears glasses is one of the most intense visual clichés of the cinema:

> The woman with glasses signifies simultaneously intellectuality and undesirability; but the moment she removes her glasses (a moment which, it seems, must always be *shown* and which is itself linked with a certain sensual quality), she is transformed into spectacle, the very picture of desire . . . The overdetermination of the image of the woman with glasses, its status as a cliché, is a crucial aspect of the cinematic alignment of structures of seeing and being seen with sexual difference. (italics in original, 1991, p. 27)

The foregrounding of Grant's "to-be-looked-at-ness" (to use Mulvey's phrase) has consequences for his role within the narrative. Beyond drawing attention to his work as an object of visual desire, Grant's characters are repeatedly placed in the narrative as objects of desire whose very desirability inspires narrative action. *Holiday* concludes when Susan follows Johnny on his holiday to Europe, uninvited but welcome. In *The Awful Truth*, Lucy masquerades as Jerry's uncouth sister in order to break his engagement and get him back. The plot of *Bringing Up Baby* is driven by the desire of Susan to make David fall in love with her, using whatever means she can. In *Only Angels Have Wings* (Howard Hawks, 1939), after seeing Geoff (Grant) at work and hearing him sing, Bonnie (Jean Arthur) abandons all of her previous plans and moves into his building in the hope he will fall in love with her. *My Favorite Wife* ends with a courtroom scene in which Ellen stages an elaborate fraud in order to get Nick to leave his new wife and return to her. In each of these stories, the desire of women for Grant's character is basically irresistible: it drives their actions and the plot completely. By providing their motivation and therefore the narrative action, Grant's ability to move the narrative, a role that Mulvey's argument places in the purview of the male, is passive: he motivates the action not through doing things but by existing as an object of desire. This tendency is at its most clear in *In Name Only*, which ends with Grant's Alec lying prostrate in hospital while his future is decided by his wife, Maida (Kay Francis) and lover, Julie (Carole Lombard), who are both standing over his bed. His narrative agency is not necessary for the film to conclude satisfactorily; in fact, his character is not even conscious at its end.

Grant's to-be-looked-at-ness and its consequent effect on the narrative in Grant's films highlights one of the key paradoxes of Hollywood stardom: the visual appeal of male stars is just as vital as that of female stars. Scholars have examined what happens when men are looked at on film. In "Masculinity as Spectacle," Steve Neale examines the representation of the male body in "male" genres such as the western and gangster film. Neale draws from

Mulvey's article to argue that in these genres, the sadism inherent in voyeurism is played out in the scenes of violence and combat: "by stopping the narrative in order to recognise the pleasure of delay, but displacing it from the male body as such and locating it more generally in the overall components of a highly ritualised scene" (1983, p. 12). He notes that during fight scenes "we are offered the spectacle of male bodies, but bodies unmarked as objects of erotic display" (p. 13). In part, this is because fight scenes tend to be both spectacle and points at which the narrative is resolved (i.e. a shoot-out) but also because "there is no cultural or cinematic convention which would allow the male body to be displayed the way that Dietrich so often is in Sternberg's films" (p. 14).

Neale argues that there are situations in which the conventions concerning looking the male body change, for example Rock Hudson in Douglas Sirk's melodramas. He writes:

> There are constant moments in these films in which Hudson is presented quite explicitly as the object of an erotic look. The look is usually marked as female. But Hudson's body is *feminised* in those moments, an indication of the strength of those conventions which dictate that only women can function as objects of an explicitly erotic gaze. (italics in original, pp. 14–15)

As outlined previously, Grant's films of his early freelance period place him in an unusual position within the gendered binary of Hollywood cinema; looked at rather than looking and acted upon rather than acting. However, despite this, he resists being feminized. Although presented as an object of visual pleasure, he is not lit softly and prettily, for example like Rock Hudson was in Sirk's films, nor is he denied agency within the narrative, as female protagonists within classical Hollywood cinema frequently were. Instead, he represents a kind of playfulness with the gender-specific rules of action and looking, desire and sexual difference. In order to explain how Cary Grant resisted feminization despite occupying a non-traditional masculine position within his films, it is necessary to look beyond the films to the extratextual discourse surrounding Grant's persona.

Steven Cohen notes that Hollywood's relationship with promoting the image of the male form is longstanding, stating that:

> Whether promoting Douglas Fairbanks Sr. and Rudolph Valentino or Robert Redford and Mel Gibson, the Hollywood studios have made it their business to sell the imagery of male stars as part of the film product, holding out to the spectator, female or male, an opportunity to take pleasure in looking at men. (1991, p. 44)

Looking at the presentation of William Holden in *Picnic* (Joshua Logan, 1955), Cohen argues that the film exploits the sight of Holden's bare chest as "the primary site of his virility" but that "it also tries to minimize that disturbing male spectacle through an extratextual institutional reliance upon Holden's star image, which exemplifies the 'basic honesty' of the American male" (p. 45). Effectively, the transgressive presentation of the visual pleasure of William Holden in *Picnic* is recuperated through the strength of his all-American star persona. The following section outlines how a similar process happens with Cary Grant through the association of his persona with the American Dream.

Recuperation and Fan Magazine Discourse

One way to determine whether strategies were used to recuperate the transgressiveness of Cary Grant's star persona is to identify the key discourses associated with his star persona in fan magazines. Fan magazines were glossy magazines that were published, usually monthly, that focused on the lives and secrets of the stars. These magazines were an integral part of studio-era Hollywood and were the main way that information about Hollywood was disseminated to fans. Regular features of fan magazines included interviews with stars, full-page color photographs or portraits of stars that could be removed and pinned up or framed, reviews of movies, gossip columns and letters to the editor. Much of the content in the magazines originated directly from the studios, for example, the articles that were purportedly penned by stars were more often written by a studio publicist (Slide, 2010).

While fan magazines provide a rich source of information about stars and how their personas were constructed, they do have some limitations as sources of analysis. The runs for the fan magazines are not often complete and the magazines themselves sometimes have pages missing. In addition to this, although it is possible to study fan magazines for an understanding of how star and star narratives were constructed in a certain way, there is no way to tell how they were read or understood by audiences at that time. Additionally, the fan magazines were marketed to a particular segment of society (white, middle-class women), which may have affected the representations of stars (Sternheimer, 2011). Therefore, in using fan magazines as data for my analysis of Cary Grant, this chapter is not attempting to determine what (if any) of the information presented within the pages is true or how this information was used by audiences; rather, it is interested in using fan magazines to identify the discourses surrounding Grant's star persona at a particular time.

As noted, upon arriving in Hollywood, all actors went through a process of transformation. This could include changing their names, taking classes such as elocution and deportment and altering physical features such as hair color, style and physique. The studio's publicity departments were a vital component of this process, and one of their biggest responsibilities was to create a fit between a star's personal life and their star persona. Cathy Klaprat describes this as convincing audiences that a star "acted identically in both her 'real' and 'reel' lives" (1985, p. 360). This process began with developing an 'authorized' biography for the star that was based largely on successful narratives from their films. This material was distributed to fan magazines, newspapers and gossip columnists. The star was assigned a publicist to handle interviews and to supervise their makeup and clothing. Glamorous portrait photos were also taken so that the studio could create an official studio image (Balio, 1995).

This process is evident from the start of Grant's career, when he was under contract to Paramount. A profile in *The New Movie Magazine* in March 1934 entitled "Once an Acrobat" (Fig 1), begins:

> Somewhere in New York City, right off Columbus Circle, the land-lady of a rooming-house is holding a trunk for non-payment of rent. The trunk belonged to a penniless young actor called Archie Leach, who doesn't exist any more [*sic*]. In his place is the handsome, confident Cary Grant of the films, the sleek, well-groomed young screen personality whose sunny countenance suggests a life singularly free from all worldly care. (Blair, 1934, p. 42)

The article continues describing how "handsome" Grant was able to "[take] poverty on the chin like the real man he was" and, through hard work and dedication, become a success. Parts of the article make it clear that Paramount struggled to find an 'authorized' biography that worked. After describing how he overcame poverty, the article states, "Neither of his parents had any connection to the stage although his grandfather, Sir Percival Leach, was famous throughout Great Britain as an actor." Sir Percival Leach did not exist. The reference to an imaginary knighted actor and the tuxedo Grant is wearing in the associated image[1] are an attempt to associate him with the kind of Britishness that had proven to be successful in the past; specifically, with 'the Hollywood Raj,' a group of British expatriate actors, including Ronald Colman, Laurence Olivier and Basil Rathbone, who were working in Hollywood in the 1930s and '40s. Sheridan Morley calls these "the respectables" and notes that they fitted easily into roles that called for upper-class gentlemen (1983, p. 129). Yet, rather than drawing on the success the

---

[1] In another example of how Hollywood publicity altered its players, in this image Grant is awkwardly holding a pen in his right hand. Grant was actually left handed.

expatriate British community were experiencing at the time, the reference to Sir Percival confused Grant's central narrative. Was he the cheerful, hardworking actor from a working class background who rose to success through hard work, or was he the grandson of an established titled actor, more connected with the upper than the working class? Understanding that his off-screen persona was supposed to be shaped to support his on-screen one, should the audience associate him with the gangster from *Gambling Ship* or the upper-class gentleman he played in *Ladies Should Listen* (Frank Tuttle, 1934)?

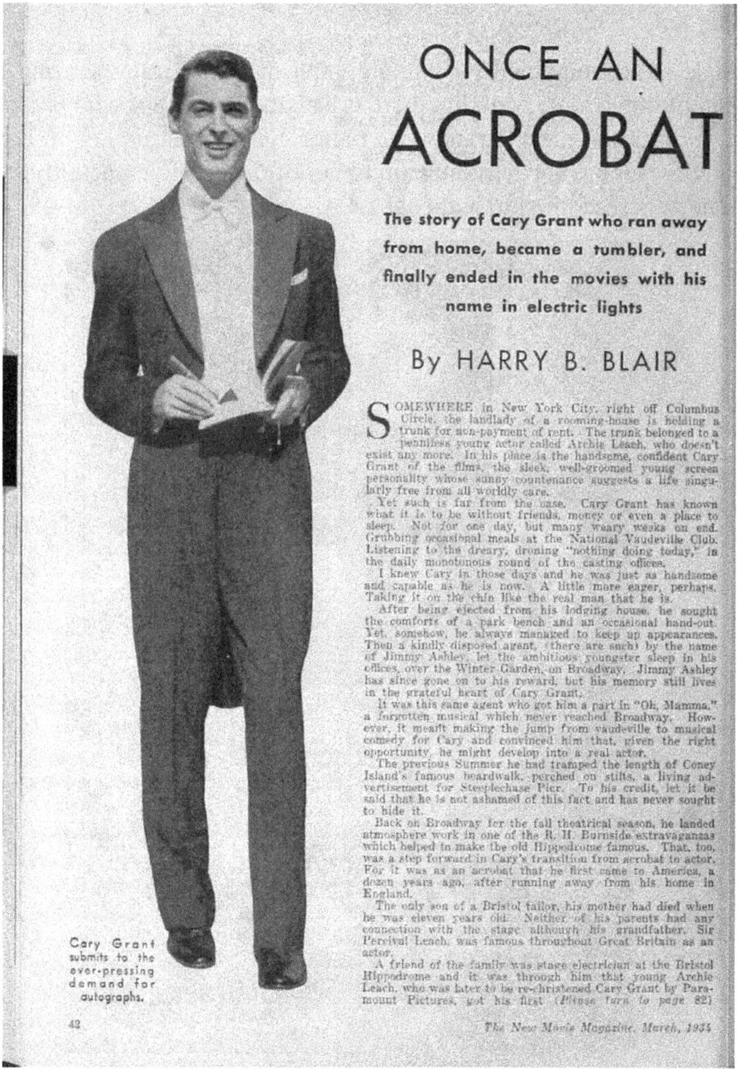

ONCE AN ACROBAT

The story of Cary Grant who ran away from home, became a tumbler, and finally ended in the movies with his name in electric lights

By HARRY B. BLAIR

SOMEWHERE in New York City, right off Columbus Circle, the landlady of a rooming-house is holding a trunk for non-payment of rent. The trunk belonged to a penniless young actor called Archie Leach, who doesn't exist any more. In his place is the handsome, confident Cary Grant of the films, the sleek, well-groomed young screen personality whose sunny countenance suggests a life singularly free from all worldly care.

Yet such is far from the case. Cary Grant has known what it is to be without friends, money or even a place to sleep. Not for one day, but many weary weeks on end. Grubbing occasional meals at the National Vaudeville Club. Listening to the dreary, droning "nothing doing today," in the daily monotonous round of the casting offices.

I knew Cary in those days and he was just as handsome and capable as he is now. A little more eager, perhaps. Taking it on the chin like the real man that he is.

After being ejected from his lodging house, he sought the comforts of a park bench and an occasional hand-out. Yet, somehow, he always managed to keep up appearances. Then a kindly disposed agent, (there are such) by the name of Jimmy Ashley, let the ambitious youngster sleep in his offices, over the Winter Garden, on Broadway. Jimmy Ashley has since gone on to his reward, but his memory still lives in the grateful heart of Cary Grant.

It was this same agent who got him a part in "Oh, Mamma," a forgotten musical which never reached Broadway. However, it meant making the jump from vaudeville to musical comedy for Cary and convinced him that, given the right opportunity, he might develop into a real actor.

The previous Summer he had tramped the length of Coney Island's famous boardwalk, perched on stilts, a living advertisement for Steeplechase Pier. To his credit, let it be said that he is not ashamed of this fact and has never sought to hide it.

Back on Broadway for the fall theatrical season, he landed atmosphere work in one of the R. H. Burnside extravaganzas which helped to make the old Hippodrome famous. That, too, was a step forward in Cary's transition from acrobat to actor. For it was as an acrobat that he first came to America, a dozen years ago, after running away from his home in England.

The only son of a Bristol tailor, his mother had died when he was eleven years old. Neither of his parents had any connection with the stage although his grandfather, Sir Percival Leach, was famous throughout Great Britain as an actor.

A friend of the family was stage electrician at the Bristol Hippodrome and it was through him that young Archie Leach, who was later to be re-christened Cary Grant by Paramount Pictures, got his first (Please turn to page 82)

Cary Grant submits to the ever-pressing demand for autographs.

42

The New Movie Magazine, March, 1934

Fig 1. "Once an Acrobat" *The New Movie Magazine* March 1934. Source: Media History Digital Library

This confusion continued in other profiles. In "He's a Fool For Cupid!", the many sides of Cary Grant are again elaborated:

> Cary Grant's not just one person. He's quintuplets, at least—all rolled into one. . . He's "moody and quiet and difficult to talk to . . . he goes suddenly 'hot' [starts performing] . . . [he's] standoffish . . . [he'd] give his friends the shirt off his back . . . [And he's] a fool for Cupid . . . There, you see, there are at least five Cary Grants. He's not just a Jekyll-Hyde sort of guy; he's the whole darn Jekyll and Hyde families! (Harmel, 1932, p. 40)

The article is accompanied by a photograph of Cary Grant wearing hunting gear and holding a gun, implying there is a sixth Cary Grant who is a big game hunter. It appears that Paramount, rather than constructing a consistent biography for Grant, were trialing a number of different character types to see which one appealed most to audiences.

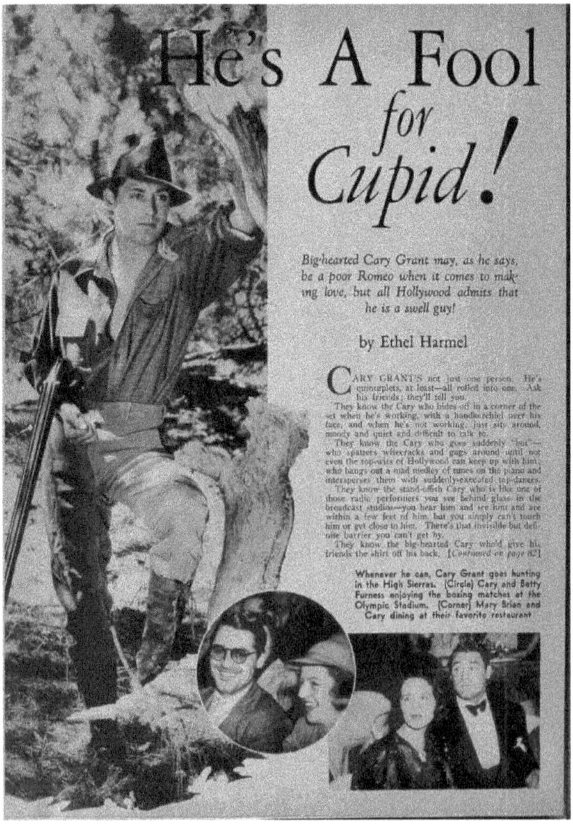
He's A Fool for Cupid!

Big-hearted Cary Grant may, as he says, be a poor Romeo when it comes to making love, but all Hollywood admits that he is a swell guy!

by Ethel Harmel

CARY GRANT'S not just one person. He's quintuplets, at least—all rolled into one. Ask his friends; they'll tell you.

They know the Cary who hides off in a corner of the set when he's working, with a handkerchief over his face, and when he's not working, just sits around, moody and quiet and difficult to talk to.

They know the Cary who goes suddenly "hot"—who spatters wisecracks and gags around until not even the top-wits of Hollywood can keep up with him; who bangs out a mad medley of tunes on the piano and intersperses them with suddenly-executed tap-dances.

They know the stand-offish Cary who is like one of those radio performers you see behind glass in the broadcast studios—you hear him and see him and are within a few feet of him, but you simply can't touch him or get close to him. There's that invisible but definite barrier you can't get by.

They know the big-hearted Cary who'd give his friends the shirt off his back. [Continued on page 82]

Whenever he can, Cary Grant goes hunting in the High Sierras. (Circle) Cary and Betty Furness enjoying the boxing matches at the Olympic Stadium. (Corner) Mary Brian and Cary dining at their favorite restaurant

Fig 2. "He's a Fool for Cupid!" *Movie Classic* 1934. Source: Media History Digital Library

After Grant went freelance, there was a clear shift in the discourses in the fan magazines. Just as his on-screen persona began to coalesce in this period, his off-screen persona likewise became to be associated with a number of consistent themes that can be identified in Grant's fan magazine discourse. Sir Percival and any claims of being an avid big game hunter vanished completely and were replaced with new, repeated themes that cohered with his on-screen persona. While not all articles contained all of the themes, they did recur throughout the articles published at this time.

One of most common themes involved an unavoidable element of his stardom: his looks. Articles frequently opened with an acknowledgement of how handsome he was. This was followed almost immediately by a firm disavowal that his handsomeness contributed to his success, instead attributing it to his talent and hard work. For example, in "Cary Grant's Secret Album," Ruth Tildesley reports:

> Kolma Flake, pretty young publicity woman, observed that Patience, the Abbe girl, had announced, on leaving, that Cary Grant was very handsome but didn't know it, as so many actors do.

> Cary blushed. Yes, believe it or not! (1937, p. 61)

In the next paragraph, she tells a story about Grant's invention of a particular lighting effect that changed the way the theatre he worked in lit scenes, implying that it was not his appearance that led to his stardom – it was his superior understanding of aspects of the performing arts. This pattern appears repeatedly in articles about Grant: an acknowledgement of his attractiveness and then an immediate dismissal of that fact followed by evidence he achieved his success through talent and hard work. In "Catching Up With Cary," Ben Maddox writes that Grant credits his success to being a freelancer and, therefore, being able to pick or reject roles. Maddox explains: "He doesn't want to rely on looks. 'What can you do with such "handsome" assignments but be a paper-mâché guy?' [Grant] asks" (1938, p. 49).

This theme exposes the same contradiction identified by Cohen earlier: a male star's visual appeal is just as important as his female counterparts' is. However, in order to disavow Grant's look as a source of success, his visual appeal first had to be acknowledged. This was very unusual for a male star at the time. This disavowal of handsomeness and avowal of hard work and talent serves two functions. Firstly, it acts to recuperate Grant's presentation as an object of visual pleasure in his films by literally denying it as a source of his appeal. These magazines acknowledge his good looks (much as the female characters in his films do) but deny they are the reason he is a star – he is a star because he is talented, works hard and is business savvy. The risks and rewards of going freelance therefore became a key part of his persona; rather than being granted stardom because of his looks, he has earned success through effort and endeavor. Being a freelance actor was thus a vital component of Grant's star image and its prominence within fan magazine discourse identifies its importance to an understanding of Cary Grant.

The second function served by referencing Grant's pathway to success is to associate Grant with one of the central myths of American society: that anyone can achieve stardom if they just work hard enough and are deserving of it. Rising from poor or ordinary origins to achieve great wealth and fame through hard work and determination is one of the central tenets of the American Dream, which Karen Sternheimer defines as:

> the deep-seated American belief that both hard work and luck can lead anyone to rise above their beginnings . . . In the mythology of the American Dream, opportunities abound and are rewarded to those the most deserving: the hardest workers, the brightest, and the most talented. (p. 8)

While the term 'American Dream' became popular during the 1930s, Sternheimer argues that the mythology behind this concept has roots in the American notion of individualism that date back to the Declaration of Independence. Celebrities personify this myth, reinforcing the idea that in American society, success is possible and that anyone who works hard enough can "make it to the top, regardless of rank" (Dyer, 1998, p. 42). As they are very public figures, stars can work as a constant reminder that success is rooted in the individual's uniqueness and determination (Sternheimer, 2011, p. 26). By repeatedly referencing Grant's rags-to-riches rise from a poor English background to an A-list star through a determination to succeed using his own effort and skills, specifically skills earned through years of training and hard work rather than innate or inherent talent, Grant's extratextual discourse works to firmly align him with the values and ideals associated with the American Dream. Fame and fortune had not been gifted to him: he deserved his success and the riches that came with him because he worked for them.

Grant's fulfilment of the American Dream was further supported through his frequently mentioned immigration from England. Not only did his journey from poverty and success support the myth of the self-made man, America had given him the opportunity that his native land had not. Many other British film stars such as Lawrence Olivier or Joan Fontaine (who, incidentally, despite being born in Japan rather than England clung resolutely to Britishness throughout her career) retained their accents to signify an elite upper-classness. Grant, in contrast, adopted a distinctive transatlantic accent that, as James Naremore describes, was "poised between two nationalities as well as between two social classes" (1990, p. 217). Neither clearly English nor American, working or upper class, Grant embodies the possibilities available to all through the myth of the American Dream.

Conclusion

Cary Grant remains one of classical Hollywood's most enduring stars, representing an ideal of romantic masculinity. However, in the early years of his career, his star persona was more closely associated with atypical or unusual masculinity than with the type of romantic leading man he is best remembered for today. This chapter tracks the development of the Cary Grant persona from contracted actor to freelance star and, in the process, identifies the key elements of Cary Grant the star text, highlighting how his persona played with the gendered norms of Hollywood cinema. At the same time, in order to minimize the transgressiveness of the masculinities he represents, recuperative strategies were employed to align him with the American Dream by highlighting and promoting the hard work involved in becoming a star. His relationship with the ideal of the American Dream was further supported by references to his poor English childhood in comparison to the riches and success available in America. Not just a romantic hero, this chapter illustrates the complexity of Grant's early star image in relation to gender, persona and national identity.

References

Balio, T. (1995). Selling stars, *Grand Design: Hollywood as a modern business enterprise, 1930-1939* (pp. 143-178). Berkeley: University of California Press.

Blair, H. B. (1934). Once an acrobat. *The new movie magazine, IX* 3, 42-94. Retrieved from Media History Digital Library.

Carman, E. S. (2008). Independent stardom: Female film stars and the studio system in the 1930s. *Women's Studies, 37*(6), 583-615. doi:10.1080/00497870802205175

Cohan, S. (1991). Masquerading as the American male in the fifties: *Picnic*, William Holden and the spectacle of masculinity in Hollywood film. *Camera Obscura, 9*(25/26), 41-72.

Doane, M. A. (1991). *Femmes Fatales: Feminism, film theory, psychoanalysis*. New York: Routledge.

Dyer, R. (1998). *Stars*. London: British Film Institute.

Ebert, R. In Memory: Cary Grant 1904-1986. Retrieved, December 17, 2017, from http://www.rogerebert.com/interviews/in-memory-cary-grant-1904-1986.

Eliot, M. (2004). *Cary Grant: the biography*. New York: Harmony Books.

Harmel, E. (1932). He's a Fool for Cupid. *Movie Classic. 11* 4, 40, 82-83. Retrieved from Media History Digital Library.

Kael, P. (2011). The man from dream city. In P. Kael & S. Schwartz (Eds.), *The age of movies: Selected writings of Pauline Kael* (pp. 465-499). New York: Library of America.

Klaprat, C. (1985). The star as market strategy: Bette Davis in another light. In T. Balio (Ed.), *The American film industry* (Rev. ed., pp. 351-376). Madison, Wisconsin: University of Wisconsin.

Lane, V. T. (1938). How Grant took Hollywood. *Photoplay. LII 5.* 22, 91. Retrieved from Media History Digital Library.

Maddox, B. (1938). Catching up with Cary. *Picture Play.* 48. Retrieved from Media History Digital Library.

Maltby, R. (2003). *Hollywood cinema* (2nd ed.). Oxford: Blackwell Publishing Ltd.

McDonald, P. (2000). *The star system: Hollywood and the production of popular identities*. London: Wallflower.

Morley, S. (1983). *Tales from the Hollywood Raj: The British film colony on screen and off.* London: Weidenfeld and Nicolson.

Mulvey, L. (1992). Visual pleasure and narrative cinema. In G. C. Mast, Marshall; Braudy, Leo (Ed.), *Film theory and criticism: introductory readings* (4th ed., pp. 746-757). Oxford: Oxford University Press.

Naremore, J. (1990). *Acting in the Cinema*. Berkeley: University of California Press.

Neale, S. (1983). Masculinity as spectacle. *Screen, 24 n6*, 2-16.

Palmer, T. (2008). Star, interrupted: The reinvention of James Stewart. In K.-P. R. Hart (Ed.), *Film and television stardom* (pp. 43-57). Middlesex: Cambridge Scholars Publishing.

Slide, A. (2010). *Inside the Hollywood fan magazine: A History of star makers, fabricators, and gossip mongers.* Jackson: University Press of Mississippi.

Sternheimer, K. (2011). *Celebrity culture and the American Dream: Stardom and social mobility*. Hoboken: Taylor & Francis.

Tildesley, R. (1937). Cary Grant's secret album. *Screenland. XXXV. 4.* 60–1, 84. Retrieved from Media History Digital Library.

Torregrossa, R. (2006). *Cary Grant: A celebration of style*. New York: Bulfinch Press.

www.ingramcontent.com/pod-product-compliance
Lightning Source LLC
Chambersburg PA
CBHW072157270326
41930CB00011B/2472